THE DEVIL

A short polemic on how to be seriously good in Court

THE DEVIL'S ADVOCATE

A short polemic on how to be seriously good in Court

Iain Morley

SWEET & MAXWELL  THOMSON REUTERS

First Edition 2005
Second Edition 2009

Published in 2009 by Sweet & Maxwell, 100 Avenue Road, London, NW3 3PF
part of Thomson Reuters (Professional) UK Limited
(Registered in England & Wales, Company No. 1679046.
Registered Office and address for service:
Aldgate House, 33 Aldgate High Street, London, EC3N 1DL.)
(http://www.sweetandmaxwell.co.uk)

Reprinted 2012
by Ashford Colour Press, Gosport, Hants

No natural forests were destroyed to make this product,
only farmed timber was used and replanted.

A CIP catalogue record for this book is available from the British Library

ISBN: 978-1-847-03768-8

ABOUT THE AUTHOR

Iain Morley is a barrister and practices in criminal law from chambers at 23 Essex Street, London. He was called to the Bar of England and Wales by Inner Temple in 1988, took Silk in 2009, and was called by the King's Inns to the Bar of Eire in 1993. He has been in a number of high profile cases in England, including the *Sarah Payne* murder in 2001. Following a period of defence pro bono work at the International Criminal Tribunal for the former Yugoslavia (ICTY) in The Hague from October 2004, he has since March 2005 been in Arusha, Tanzania, assisting the United Nations to prosecute the 1994 Rwandan genocide of the Tutsi by the Hutu at the International Criminal Tribunal for Rwanda (ICTR), where he has appeared in four cases concerning six significant defendants. He is at present a well-known practitioner in the law and evidence of genocide and crimes against humanity.

He read law at Lady Margaret Hall in Oxford, and while at Bar School in 1988 won the World Universities Debating Championships in Sydney, Australia.

Since 1992, he has been a member of the Inner Temple Advocacy Committee, where he has trained bar students, pupils and junior tenants in advocacy skills. As an advocacy teacher, he has an "A grade" listing within the Inns of Court, and has constructed and run various advocacy courses. He has also taught junior and senior members of his Inn in how to teach advocacy.

Outside the Inn, he has taught advocacy skills to City solicitors, and to visiting lawyers from the EU in London, from the EU in the Netherlands, regularly at the ICTR, to Polish lawyers and visiting Judges from the former USSR in Warsaw, and to lawyers from throughout the former Soviet sphere in Germany who wish to practise at the International Criminal Court.

Presently he lives in Tanzania.

ACKNOWLEDGEMENTS
For the second edition

I would very much like to acknowledge assistance in the final drafts of this short work from the following:

His Honour Judge Richard MacGregor Johnson and Joanna Korner QC—both Masters of the Inner Temple Bench and former Chairpersons of the Inner Temple Advocacy Committee.

Mr Justice Christopher Floyd, His Honour Judge Toby Hooper QC, and Charles George QC—all Masters of the Inner Temple Bench and members of the Inner Temple Advocacy Committee.

Kenneth Aylett—Master of the Inner Temple Bench, member of the Inner Temple Advocacy Committee, and one who in the past has suggested I write this book.

Oscar Del Fabbro, Stephen Hellman, and Gareth Branston—barristers practising in criminal law.

Michael Hall—former law lecturer at the University of Oxford and presently in practice at the Bar in Sydney.

Alexander Kleanthous—solicitor in civil practice.

Leslie Cuthbert—a former partner in a leading London criminal solicitors, and one whose enthusiasm as a practising criminal solicitor for this work was very encouraging.

Stephen Rapp, presently the Prosecutor for the Special Court in Sierra Leone, who while Chief of Prosecutions at the UN International Criminal Tribunal for Rwanda in Arusha, suggested I add a chapter on international criminal practice.

Lady Justice Ines Monica Weinberg de Roca, Judge at the ICTR, and a designated Appeals Judge for both the ICTR and ICTY, who helpfully reviewed the new chapter on international practice.

And finally Nicola Thurlow, the publisher with Sweet and Maxwell, who in late 2004 patiently listened to my suggestion this book would sell, was persuaded, and put it on the bookshelves.

THE DEVIL'S ADVOCATE

A short polemic on how to be seriously good in Court

CHAPTERS

CHAPTER I

THIS BOOK

This book will take you three hours to read.

I hope you may never forget it.

I hope you will come back to it time and again.

Keep it for reference.

It's been published in a small size so you can carry it about.

It is full of good ideas which in the early years of your practice, you can dip into while thinking of what to do in a case.

With reading it, your advocacy will probably improve immediately.

It's almost guaranteed.

This is not a reasoned academic text. It is a polemic. It is about being good in court—no messing, no guff, no clever arguments, no tedious endless proofs and justifications. It tells it as it is.

It's about how to do the job really well.

***

And it applies to all advocates of up to five years experience.

It is designed to be read easily by anyone interested in becoming an effective advocate, whether presently at school, in university, at law school, or in the early stages of doing the job at the Bar or as a solicitor.

It is written with crime in mind. But many of the rules apply to the courtroom in civil practice too.

The book will make sense wherever the justice system is adversarial. Much of what is in this book has been or is being taught in Scotland, Ireland, India, South Africa, Hong Kong, Australia, Kenya, New Zealand, Canada, and the USA. Many of the techniques are being embraced by the formerly communist countries of Eastern Europe. The rules of advocacy are travelling widely.

I've written it in pretty much my style of speech from when I teach advocacy students. The book should read like I am talking to you, with colour and enthusiasm. It shouldn't feel like you are reading. I am hoping the style will be effective in communicating what may otherwise be a series of rather dull rules. My apologies if I appear to over-egg it in places, and drive you a bit nuts! But at least, you'll probably remember what's been said.

Where I refer to an advocate or judge, I will use the expression "he" as being I hope gender neutral.

You won't agree with everything you read.

Good.

At least you're thinking.

Thinking about advocacy.

What works and what doesn't.

And why.

The book is called *"The Devil's Advocate"* because it may make you see advocacy from a new perspective.

Your assumptions will be challenged.

***

Each page will contain one or two thoughts, no more. Some pages will therefore be short.

Some of them very short.

Like this one.

Try not to fly through the book.

Instead, think about each page as you read it. Lodge each thought in your mind.

Don't skim. Think.

***

As for myself, I don't pretend I can do advocacy right every time in court, but I think I've come across what works. And I know I will always be learning.

***

Chapter II

LEARNING ADVOCACY

Advocacy is a skill.

The skill of persuasion.

Like *any* skill, **ADVOCACY CAN BE LEARNT**.

Up to a point.

No one can be taught to be a brilliant advocate, just as no one can be taught to be a brilliant pianist. Brilliance requires talent. Whether any of us have talent is in the gift of the Gods.

However, we can be **TAUGHT COMPETENCE** in advocacy.

Competence is not making errors.

We can be taught how not to make errors.

Simply that. No more complicated than that. No errors.

Just as most people can be taught to play the piano, so too can they be taught advocacy. An error-free performance on the piano, like perhaps a youngster playing Beethoven's fairly simple "*Fur Elise*", is creditable, will raise murmurs of approval, and generally cannot be hugely criticised. The youngster may not be destined to be a brilliant pianist, but an error-free Fur Elise is something most youngsters can be taught to play, even if a little woodenly.

In the same way, we can learn an error-free performance in court.

But unlike the pianist, an error-free performance in court is something more—

It is highly unusual.

Advocacy without errors is no small achievement.

***

As with any skill, **PRACTICE** is what is necessary.

***

Reading books like this will be perfectly useless in the absence of practice.

We learn advocacy by doing.

So practice.

Practice. Practice. Practice.

The ideas in this book are for trying out. If something does not work for you, form that opinion after you have tried it and not before. There will be suggestions you disagree with, but what we must avoid is an armchair debate. **TRY THINGS OUT**, then debate them, not beforehand.

Advocacy should involve experimenting.

Regularly.

Trying to **IMPROVE** existing skills.

Trying to create **NEW** skills.

Don't sit around. Get up and do.

Practice in front of the mirror. Practice in front of friends. Practice to and from work in the quiet of your mind on the train. Always be looking for ways of phrasing questions, turning phrases, encapsulating arguments, controlling witnesses, and more, and so on. Think new ideas and in time have the courage to try them.

***

It is astonishing how few students and advocates have ever read an **ADVOCACY BOOK**.

There are large academic texts available from the USA, which are sometimes avoided, because they can appear intimidating. However, they can be very good.

Try *"Fundamental Trial Techniques"* by Thomas Mauet. It's a bit heavy, but very thorough, and has loads of ideas.

And of course, there are many thinner contributions which offer advice, and particularly which quote from brilliant past cases. The cross-examination of Wilde by Carson is a powerful read. Snippets of other less famous cases are instructive and often amazing.

Surely every advocate should have read:

    Richard Du Canns'   *"The Art of the Advocate"*

    Francis Wellman's   *"The Art of Cross-examination"*

Just for starters.

Have a look for them now.

***

The modest aim of this book is to teach you competence.

I am hoping after you have absorbed the ideas here, and then put them into practice, you will play advocacy's Fur Elise without mistakes, even if a little woodenly at first.

It will then be up to you how good you get after you've learned Fur Elise, and in time, as you become more sophisticated and fluent on the advocacy keyboard, you will learn for yourself whether you have the talent of an Edward Carson, or Marshall Hall or Clarence Darrow.

But before we can run, we must walk.

***

CHAPTER III

TRUTH

This is a tricky area.

Rightly or wrongly, adversarial advocacy is not really an enquiry into the truth.

Perhaps the adversarial system should be about finding out what really happened. But it isn't. Instead it creates a polite contest.

The contest is this: while a judge or a jury will seek out the truth as best they can, the advocates use their skill to test the evidence, and to control the way the evidence emerges, and then comment in closing on whether a case has been proved to the necessary standard of proof.

Perhaps it should not be like this, but in reality this is what happens.

What is the truth of an incident? Truth of course is a large concept. Philosophers have written about it for thousands of years. Many would say there is no objective truth, that there are really only different perspectives. However, if there is an objective truth, unfortunately courts do not always find it.

***

I'm only saying what the reality is. I'm not trying to be controversial. I'm saying it as it is, as I promised. No guff. No philosophising.

And the truth is that adversarial advocacy is not really an enquiry into the truth. It is a well-mannered contest, in which there are rules, and it is possible to win, even in the face of seemingly overwhelming evidence if you play the rules better than your opponent, and learn to be a more persuasive advocate than your opponent.

The system is supposed to work on the assumption the advocates are evenly balanced, and so they cancel each other out, leaving the tribunal to consider the evidence after it has been examined. But the flaw in the theory is that advocates can have uneven skills, and usually do.

Your job is always to try to be more skilful in the art of advocacy than your opponent.

A good advocate can win a weak case, particularly if against a less able advocate.

In court, there is acting, and there are games of strategy. Maybe there should not be, but there are, every day, up and down the country.

Witnesses often exaggerate in order to win, admitting no failings for fear they will damage their case.

And encouraging the witnesses, or against the witnesses, are the advocates, whose job is not to give up, even when it seems hopeless. **ADVOCATES TRY TO WIN THEIR CASES WITHIN THE RULES, IRRESPECTIVE OF THE TRUTH**, irrespective of that hopelessness. And often it is never entirely hopeless for the skilful advocate.

Lawyers praise advocates who have succeeded with weak cases, not as a mark of the truth having triumphed, but as a celebration of the advocate's skill.

And remember, cases will often turn on what evidence within the rules an advocate has skilfully managed to keep suppressed.

Often, it can be more important when questioning witnesses to **KNOW WHAT NOT TO ASK**, to know what areas will get you into trouble with the witness, and so avoid them.

So there it is—rightly or wrongly, an advocate's job is not actually about truth. It is important to understand this, sad or illogical as it may seem, right from the outset of the advocate's career.

If not about truth, what then?

***

CHAPTER IV

WINNING

Being an advocate is about **WINNING WITHIN THE RULES**.

Perhaps it shouldn't be.

But it is.

The goal is to win;

the means of winning is by being persuasive.

We each strive, and should strive, to win, but always, always, always within the rules.

There are the rules of evidence and the rules of law. You are assumed to know these. Nothing more will be said about them here.

It appears to me there are also three primary professional rules.

These are really about attitudes of mind. I am not trying here to rewrite the Codes of Conduct for solicitors or for the Bar. The Codes need careful reading and you are assumed to know them. I am simply emphasising the seemingly most important beacons of integrity which ought to burn bright in every lawyer, and should guide the way we think.

And I think there are three beacons.

They are commandments of behaviour.

***

The first is **THOU SHALT NOT MISLEAD THE COURT**.

You are assumed to know this.

It is a long subject and will have been studied at law school.

Always remember to consult colleagues and if necessary your professional body telephone help-line, which you ought to know off by heart, if in any doubt.

Always consult.

Misleading the court is serious misconduct and will, and rightly should, lead to formal proceedings of censure.

For God's sake, don't lie. Even if it means you will win the case and you think no one will find out. Don't ever say something you **KNOW IS NOT TRUE**. Ever. And I mean **EVER**. If you tell one lie, and by this I don't mean mentioning something which may not be true, which is unclear, but instead you **KNOW** it, **KNOW KNOW KNOW IT**, no matter how small a teeny weeny lie, you should never step into court again. **NEVER EVER AGAIN**.

Witnesses might lie. Criminal defendants often lie. But an officer of the court—and that's what you are—is upon his honour, and never ever ever ever lies. You must be trustworthy to the judge, to the jury, to your colleagues, as without this you cannot be persuasive, and if you are caught out on just one occasion, no one will ever believe you again. May the ground open and swallow you, may lightening bolts cascade from the Heavens, may the monsters of Hades surface and drag you down to Hell's darkest dungeon, if you do it even once.

Just don't do it.

I won't say anymore about it as it is so huge an issue, it need only simply be mentioned to make the point of how important it is.

***

The second rule however is not such a formal one. But is it pretty much just as important. **THOU SHALT NOT USE SHARP PRAC-TICE WITH YOUR COLLEAGUES**.

This is a difficult area. You have a duty to the client. But equally, that duty cannot be fulfilled if you are sharp with your colleagues as they won't trust you, and this will make running your case to the advantage of the client very difficult.

We are not talking about lying here. We are talking about being nasty, evasive, weasily, too clever by half, mealy-mouthed, disingenuous, and manipulative.

ACT WITH HONOUR.

Generally, the trick is it is better to refuse to be drawn on what you will do, it is better to say nothing and make it clear you are saying nothing, than to say you will do one thing and then do another. If you say you will do something, then do it; if you say you will not do something, then don't do it.

If you wish to raise a matter of law, give your opposition at least some notice. If you have legal authorities on which you will rely, alert the opposition early, not at the moment of submission.

It is often a question of how it's done, not what is done.

Be Henry V not Richard III.

***

Maintain **POLITENESS AND CLARITY**.

A rule of thumb is it is best to deal with your opposition, as you would want them to deal with you.

Why not confound them?

The answer is clear. As advocates, we spend our working lives together. Clients usually come but once or twice. However, we encounter each other all the time. It is professional suicide to have a reputation for being sharp. Reputation travels quickly. Lawyers love to gossip. There will come a time when meeting a new advocate, we see eyes narrow, and inexplicably co-operation is withdrawn. Sadly they have heard about us.

In Britain and Ireland, and most of the Commonwealth and Common Law world, we rightly pride ourselves on the level of co-operation between advocates against each other. Outside court, decisions are taken which speed up the smooth running of trials and allow the parties and the court to focus quickly on the real issues.

Long may this continue. Don't blow it by being sharp.

Please don't confuse this with selling your client out to keep in with your lawyer friends. This is not what is being suggested. Your duty to your client is paramount, but remember, it must be within the rules. The rules require you do not mislead the court. In the same way, there is an unspoken rule you do not deliberately mislead your colleagues.

Don't lie. Don't u-turn on what you have promised, without very, very good reason which you must then explain fully. Don't say things intending to renege on them later. As I say, it is better to say nothing, and point out you are saying nothing, than to say something you later change.

***

The third rule is **THOU SHALT ALWAYS TRY TO THINK LIKE THE TRIBUNAL**.

Why? Because if you do this, you will automatically become less partisan.

Being perceived to be less partisan is really very important. You will become more reliable in the eyes of the judge or jury and your later arguments are more likely to succeed.

There is all the difference in the world between representing someone and taking sides. Your job is the former, not in the style of B-movies being a hired gun.

You should try to take decisions with this thought in mind: *"What should the judge do about this problem?"*, or *"what is the jury likely to make of the general circumstances of this case, or appearance of the defendant, or the presentation of his mother as a character witness?"*

The thought should not be:

>   *"What would I like the judge to do?"*

nor is it

>   *"I wonder if I can get this past the jury?"*

nor is it

>   *"I'll have a go"*.

Or another way of looking at it is ask yourself:

>   *"If I were the tribunal, what would I think?"*

The thing to avoid here is trying to think like the client. You are paid to predict and influence what will happen in court. Whoever it is, be it a burglar, the local constabulary, a multi-million pound business, the client wants you to think for him. And he wants you to work out what will best serve his interests while he lies in the power of the court.

However, there is sometimes a tension created by the client appearing to tell the advocate what he wants done in court. Remember, without becoming arrogant, you will usually know what is best for the client if you can develop an understanding of how the tribunal thinks. If we all did everything clients insisted upon, court could descend into a circus.

Your job is to straddle the fine line between pleasing the client and pleasing the court. Pleasing the court will usually benefit the client. Don't roll over, but at the same time don't undermine the entire courtroom process by becoming the unthinking mouthpiece of a difficult or inexperienced client. If you can anticipate the way the tribunal is thinking, you can craft so much of your presentation to meet its expectation, and soothe its concerns. You are the one with the training. Don't forget it.

**

If we follow the rules, then within their constraint, it is your job to win.

The constraining rules are the rules of law and evidence, the codes of conduct, and the rules of advocacy. You're assumed to know the rules of law and evidence. You're assumed to know the codes of conduct. But you'll be learning the rules of advocacy throughout your whole career.

So, within those rules, it is your job to win.

But not at any cost. Keep the three beacons burning.

And with them burning, now you must fight your case. And really fight it. Simply detachedly presenting the case is insufficient. An advocate must try to be totally committed. Of course, we may lose in the end, but it will be fearlessly, bright-eyed, and not for want of trying.

And remember. There are some who will say expansively with an easy smile they are not interested in winning, but just in presenting the evidence. It is a fashionable thing to say. It makes them seem harmless.

Don't believe a word of it.

***

CHAPTER V

TRIBUNAL PSYCHOLOGY

A tribunal has power.

The power of decision.

It decides who wins.

You don't.

The decision is not yours to make. It is theirs. And the tribunal will jealously guard its power to decide. An advocate must always avoid appearing to instruct a tribunal on what decision to reach. Instruction is completely wrong.

Our job is not to *tell* it what to think;

Our job is to *show* it what to think.

The difference between telling and showing is monumentally huge. Learn this difference immediately.

People who tell, instruct.

People who show, assist.

No one likes being told what to do.

But everyone likes **ASSISTANCE**.

Advocates should try to ensure the tribunal sees them as assistance. It is much easier to persuade people who believe you are helping them. Avoid being seen as a gladiator. It is difficult to persuade people who believe you are locked in a contest with them. Be wary of being seen to be against the judge, or the opposition advocate, or the witnesses: that is how you become seen as a gladiator.

Of course you are for one side or the other and trying to win within the rules. But try not to let it show. Keep the word "assistance" at the forefront of your presentation to the tribunal.

***

The word assistance goes further. We should project the notion we are a **FACILITATOR**.

A facilitator is an advocate who makes it easier for the tribunal to agree with our case.

Imagine yourself as a guide. We show the tribunal the way home. We facilitate its journey. We make it easy to follow our route.

***

Another word to have at the forefront of your mind is this,
unquestionably this,
undeniably,
irrefutably,
hugely
this—

IRRESISTIBLE.

Make the route by which you guide the tribunal home *irresistible*.

Make it so that they cannot help but willingly and happily agree with you.

Always
always
always
look for a quality of irresistibility in your arguments. It is the hallmark of a truly great advocate.

It cannot be emphasised enough.

A great advocate is not one who argues loudly and with noticeably great intellect. Rather, it is the one who says things which seem right. Simple. Easy. Just plain right.

It is as if the advocate is not there. There is only the argument. And the answer to the argument is obvious . . . But of course it wasn't obvious, until the irresistible advocate explained why, and makes it look as if there was never an argument in the first place.

***

IRRESISTIBLE.

YOU'RE NOT A GLADIATOR.

DON'T PUSH—INVITE.

DON'T FROGMARCH THE TRIBUNAL—QUIETLY SHOW THE WAY.

***

Don't forget it!

***

Again, these are expressions I just don't want you to miss.

Sorry if I'm repeating myself.

I'm trying to drill these very important thoughts into your mind.

Some people think being an advocate is about pushing, about forcing everyone to agree with you, whether they like it or not.

It's not about that at all.

As I say, don't push.

Coax the tribunal, invite it, but never demand.

If you push, it will probably push back.

> *"You must agree that . . . "*
> —*"Oh yeah, must we?"*
> *"You will find the defendant guilty . . . "*
> —*"No we won't."*

Cloak everything as an **INVITATION**. It amounts to pushing your case, but so much more effectively because it does not look as if you are pushing.

> *"It may be you agree . . . "*
> —*"Of course we do"*
> *"It is my invitation to you to find him not guilty".*
> —*"Nicely put, we'll think about it favourably".*

***

Never forget about **LOSS OF FACE**.

Tribunal loss of face. Not yours. Your pride is expendable.

Don't embarrass them. Always allow an escape route for the tribunal to save face.

If you seek a favourable ruling on a matter where the judge has already given preliminary indications on how the judicial mind is working, then be aware the judge may find it difficult to agree with you if your application embarrasses his previous thinking.

This is only human nature. Tribunals are human too.

Provide **ESCAPE ROUTES**. It may be a new piece of evidence can be proffered as the reason to change the judicial mind.

This is better than simply asserting the judge is wrong.

If, as sometimes happens, a view has been expressed by the judge before you have addressed the court, then **BLAME YOURSELF**.

Tell the judge you apologise for not having raised the matter earlier, or were not fully concentrating on events—whatever, as long as you provide a save-face mechanism so that the judge can change his mind without looking as if there has been a judicial u-turn.

Don't take them on. You'll lose. Assist them.

Don't fight them. Everything is your fault—never theirs.

***

There you have it. That's how you facilitate a tribunal irresistibly to agree with you so you can win your case within the rules, irrespective of the truth of matters.

So, you're not trying to be a tub-thumper.

You should be looking to become an irresistible facilitator.

So where does irresistible facilitating come from?

It comes from the skill of persuasiveness.

***

CHAPTER VI

PERSUASIVENESS

Advocacy is the skill of persuasion.

Your job is to persuade the tribunal of your case.

Not to shout at them.

Or moan.

Or complain.

Or be terribly clever.

Persuade.

What is persuasiveness?

How do we measure it?

Are there techniques to improve it?

***

What is persuasiveness?

An advocate is persuasive if the tribunal prefers his case when weighed against the burden and standard of proof.

We'll say that again.

AN ADVOCATE IS PERSUASIVE IF THE TRIBUNAL PREFERS HIS CASE WHEN WEIGHED AGAINST THE BURDEN AND STANDARD OF PROOF.

Notice persuasiveness is not simply where his case is preferred.

Right at the core of persuasiveness is the burden and standard of proof. A jury may prefer a prosecution witness, but cannot be sure beyond reasonable doubt; they may prefer the prosecution case, so that they think it highly probably right, but with the burden on the prosecution to prove the case so that they are sure, not what is highly probable, in the final analysis it does not matter who the jury prefer—the defence still wins.

So an advocate must firstly **IDENTIFY TO WHAT STANDARD MUST THE TRIBUNAL BE PERSUADED**.

In crime, for the prosecutor, his case must be beyond reasonable doubt. For the defence, his case must simply be reasonably possible.

Advocates are often heard talking to each other about cases, and it is clear no one is thinking about the burden and standard of proof. Prosecutors sometimes say their case is clearly the more obvious explanation. But is it the only explanation? That's the real question. The defence sometimes worry the jury will find it hard to believe the defendant in evidence. But is the jury *sure* the defendant is lying? That may be the real question. And remember, it is more difficult for a jury to say they are sure someone is lying, than for them to say simply they find it hard to believe him, which of course is not the same thing.

Think about this.

In how many speeches have we heard a prosecutor invite a tribunal to consider that an injury is consistent with the allegation of a punch. Yet the more precise issue is whether the injury can only be explained by a punch. Is it equally consistent, as the defence suggest, with a blow from tripping over?

Or even, is it merely possibly consistent?

Is it enough to persuade the tribunal if the prosecutor simply says the injury is consistent with his case?

No.

***

How is persuasiveness measured?

By getting the tribunal to **REALLY, REALLY, REALLY THINK ABOUT YOUR CASE**.

Advocates cannot win every case.

Some are just bad cases.

Some are good cases spoiled by bad witnesses.

Some cases are won without the tribunal having to give it much thought—lawyers often say these cases resolve themselves and that advocates were actually unnecessary.

But most cases do require advocates to be persuasive. What may seem obvious can be turned upside down by a persuasive advocate, because he persuades the tribunal to *really, really think* about his case.

Don't believe advocates when they say they don't think advocates have much influence and everything depends on the witnesses—they are either being modest, or they are not very good. Skilful questioning and a well-planned closing speech can turn the world on its head.

Or at the very least, it will get the tribunal to really, really, really think.

***

As for techniques to improve persuasiveness, there are many.
They can be learnt.

Generally, but not always, they work.

**

We start with **PERSONAL PRESENTATION**.

Every advocate is a salesperson, selling a client's story. This may sound unattractive. But it's true. And what's worse is very often the story you have to sell is seemingly unsellable. So you have to be a very good salesperson—not just any old salesperson.

There follow some mindlessly obvious suggestions, which although obvious, are often ignored. They shouldn't be.

DRESS WELL. Obvious isn't it?

Neat hair, dark clothing, like for a funeral or job interview. Don't get slack about your appearance at court. Every day you are on show. So show them. Make sure the clothes you wear make you look formal and fantastic.

Looking fantastic makes you *LOOK LIKE A WINNER*. Tribunals can't help themselves—they take people who look like winners very seriously. And you have not opened your mouth yet. Elementary human psychology.

There is something else mindlessly so obvious you will grin—wear expensive polished shoes. For inexplicable reasons, polished expensive shoes carry serious weight. People often look down during negotiation, when talking with clients or the opposition, probably to avoid appearing threatening, and when they do so, they see each other's shoes. It is surprising how often shoes are remembered, particularly if messy.

My polished shoes suggestion from the first edition has raised a touch of mirthful feedback, but I really do stand by it. I have never forgotten from being in the school play that line from Arthur Miller's Death of a Salesman: *"With a smile and a shoeshine, the whole world is yours"*. He's basically right. And he married Marilyn Monroe, so he must know a thing or two.

White or light shirts are preferred. Too much colour and you will give the impression you fancy yourself (which you may do—most lawyers do, but you must hide it). If a tribunal thinks you fancy yourself, it will often instinctively turn against you.

So now you look like a winner.

Behaving like one comes next.

***

The most important person in court, besides the judge is of course the usher.

THE USHER.

The usher controls the list and will usually decide when your case will be called. If you are rude or high-handed, not only will your case slip to the back of the list, but the opinion of the usher on your behaviour often gets reported to the clerk of the court who may report it to the judge as part of the courtroom gossip that inevitably is generated where there are people, personalities, and pressure. You don't want your judge thinking ill of you before he has even seen you.

The skills of advocacy begin not when the tribunal sits. They begin when you arrive at court. In everything you do, you are on show. You are on show to the client, to the clerk, to the public, to the usher. If you look like a winner, remember to behave well, and not like a prima-donna.

And what you need next is very important.

***

POISE.

***

Poise. Poise. Poise. Poise.

***

Always remember poise.

Maybe I am overdoing the poise thing. I'm trying to get you to remember it above many of the other things I am saying. It is very important. Carry yourself meaningfully and **DO NOT BE AFRAID TO OCCUPY SPACE** in the courtroom. Your movements should be purposeful. Hold your head up.

Do not let your head sink into your chest, your body sliding into smallness, forward on the seat, so that you occupy less space, look bored, and appear to be a sloth.

Just holding your head up makes a huge difference. Whether leaning on elbows, reclining a little in the seat, addressing the tribunal, whatever—with a head held up, you will look attentive and in control. Obvious isn't it. And you still haven't opened your mouth yet.

***

FIDDLING comes in many forms. Avoid it. Don't play with pens. Try not to doodle, even though the urge can sometimes be overwhelming—someone will spot you. Don't pull at your suit while addressing the tribunal. Don't rock backwards and forwards while seated or upright. Don't shuffle papers while talking—it is irritating and will only mess up your bundle.

Many of us are unaware of fiddling, but it is obvious to everyone else. Ask your opponent if you might be a fiddler, and be prepared for an embarrassing but ultimately extremely helpful criticism.

Even better, video yourself. See if you aren't amazed. Go on—try it.

***

HANDS should not be in pockets as this looks too casual. Put them behind your back. Or put papers in them, or papers in one and a pen in the other, or papers in one and the other behind your back. Or put them both on the lectern.

Hands are a nuisance. They become barriers. We hide from the witness or judge by putting them to our face, under our chin, folded across our chest, even to our mouth, to our earlobes, scratching our nose. We fidget, and the body language speaks unknown to us directly to the tribunal.

Generally, our uncontrolled hands say unpleasant things.

They can suggest embarrassment, perhaps lack of faith in the case, and weakness. And so then we are ignored by the tribunal.

Stand straight up, head held up, hands controlled, relish the space you occupy, and enjoy the attention of the entire court.

If you have to fidget to relieve the tension, furiously *wriggle your toes*. Crazy but true. It is unseen, requires considerable effort, and uses such concentration that there is no room left for your brain while addressing the court and wriggling toes to indulge in any visible involuntary fiddling. Daft as it may sound, this really is a tiptop tip.

***

DON'T HIDE. It is easy to scrunch up over a lectern, or allow shoulders to bend forward and the head to hang while addressing the court.

What you are doing is hiding.

You are trying to occupy the smallest amount of space.

You are showing you are afraid.

Whether you are afraid or not, don't show it.

Relish your space. Say to yourself: I will stand like a rock, and let the winds blow and the seas foam all about me, but I shall stand. This is not arrogance. It is simply being solid.

***

MAKE EYE CONTACT with the tribunal.

Be the tribunal lay magistrates

or   a district judge

or   a circuit judge

or   a jury

or   the High Court

or   the Court of Appeal,

MAKE EYE CONTACT.

This cannot be stressed enough.

So it will be said again: make eye contact.

Look at your judge. Look at each member of the jury.

Many advocates look down, avoiding eye contact, particularly with judges.

But judges are people too.

Talk to them, rather than to your notes. Advocacy is not some intellectual abstraction: it is about persuading people.

No one ever persuaded anyone of anything by talking down at the floor.

So if it helps, hold your notes close to your head, at chest height, rather than leaving them on the bench so you can occasionally hide by looking down. Close to your head, you can glance at them, follow them, and yet maintain eye contact, so that the dreadful hiding thing is minimised.

And of course by holding your notes, you have something to do with those damned hands.

***

When speaking, **SPEAK FROM YOUR LUNGS**, not from the back of your throat.

The voice is more powerful from the lungs and carries further, without sounding as if it is a shout. Also, the voice is **DEEPER**. Deeper voices sound more persuasive—why, is a mystery, but they just do. Tinny, light voices can sound plaintive, weak, sometimes desperate, appear to be shouts, sound out of control, and finally and most importantly, are difficult to listen to, and so in the end they can be ignored.

A deeper voice is also naturally **SLOWER** in delivery. This does not mean it proceeds at a snail's pace. Rather it is simply easier to consume and understand its content. Just how slow is good is a subject for later, but for the moment, as a general principle, slow is better than fast.

***

Leaning forward at **84.5 DEGREES** to the perpendicular was once said as a comic aside to be the optimum angle at which to stand to be the most persuasive.

***

Funny or not, it is true.

84.5 degrees, or thereabouts.

If you stand bolt upright at 90 degrees, the impression can exist you are leaning backwards. Or standing somewhat aloof.

However, leaning slightly forward conveys a wish to engage the tribunal, while appearing solid, dispassionate, with a firmness of purpose about your address: we look like we believe what we are saying to be correct, are sensible and reliable, and really want what we are saying to be fully understood.

This may sound the weirdest suggestion you have ever read.

It probably is.

But it works.

Try it.

***

So where are we?

We have not opened our mouth yet, but already we have the court's
full attention:

> we dress well,
>
> keep our head up,
>
> do not hide,
>
> we have control of our hands,
>
> we move purposefully,
>
> our voice is a bit deeper and slower,
>
> we have eye contact,
>
> we stand like a rock,
>
> at the optimum angle.

We look **CONFIDENT**. We may in fact be worried, feeling awkward,
and uneasy. How we feel does not matter, as long as we don't show it.

Feign confidence.

And the techniques applied so far will have helped do just that.

The tribunal has the impression we will be persuasive.

Now we open our mouth.

***

PERSONALITY comes next.

Once you open your mouth, people start forming judgements.

Please do not try to be someone you are not.

Advocates need only remember the rules of law, evidence and conduct, good manners and at all times deference to the judge.

Within these constraints, **BE YOURSELF**.

There is no need to change your accent. If you normally gesticulate, within reason use gestures where helpful. Vary your tone and pace, just as you would in conversation.

Project yourself, not just the case.

This is an area which often troubles advocates. On the one hand, a court is not a coffee morning, ripe for cheery chat and easy banter. But on the other hand, all around you are real people. Real people relate to each other through their personalities. A court will best relate to you through yours.

Advocacy is not a science—it is an art. It does not work to hide our personalities behind passionless question structures, and carefully prepared legal submissions. A correctly phrased question to a witness, if delivered boringly and in a monotone, will usually have nothing like its intended effect. So much more is communicated by you as a person than simply what you say: people look at how you say it, with what tone, with what expressions, and with what body language.

***

Try listening to an argument with your eyes closed.

***

It is immediately apparent that quite a lot of vitality is lost but at least you have tone to consider.

Now try listening to a computer (as some now can do) speaking in monotone, with your eyes closed.

It is a nightmare.

A case is not just about witnesses and the evidence.

It is also about you.

You are speaking for someone.

If you try to be somebody you are not, you will lack credibility. Without credibility, you cannot be persuasive.

Be yourself.

Project yourself through variation of the tone of your voice. **VOICE VARIATION** gives you personality and makes it easier to listen to you.

***

Now we come to a very difficult area in the art of persuasiveness—
BEING LIKED.

***

If it is possible,
and it is not always possible in some cases,
an advocate should try to be liked by the tribunal.

People are more sympathetic to those they like: it is human nature.
With a sympathetic hearing, there is more opportunity to be
persuasive.

Being liked by your opposition is quite helpful too: it is easier to
plan out the case together, to avoid sudden surprises, and occasionally to persuade your opposition to agree evidence which will be to
your advantage.

However, being liked is nowhere near as important as putting you
client's interests first.

If there is a conflict between being liked and your client's interests,
then put your client's interests first.

***

NEVER, EVER, EVER PUT BEING LIKED AHEAD OF THE CLIENT'S INTERESTS.

***

EVER.

This may sound obvious, but it can be difficult in practice. We can be intimidated by senior opposition or a difficult judge. The unspoken suggestion may be that we should roll over and play dead if we want to remain friendly. The suggestion may even be we cannot be any good as advocates, unless we concede some point, which surely is obvious to someone with real ability.

Be very careful.

You now need **JUDGEMENT**.

Judgement is what you are paid for. You must have this if you are to be any good. It is your greatest necessity as a lawyer. Whether you have it or not is usually a question of talent, feel, common sense, understanding of the law, experience and occasionally cunning. It cannot be taught.

We must each have the confidence to form our own judgements on issues.

We must each have the talent to get it right more often than not.

Each advocate can be (and usually is) different on the precise view to be taken on some point. If in your judgement a point must be taken, listen carefully to your judge, listen carefully to your opposition, consult others, but if your judgement remains the same, and you risk not being liked for it, follow your judgment not your popularity.

***

FOLLOW YOUR JUDGEMENT, NOT YOUR POPULARITY.

***

Of course this is obvious, but it can be very difficult to do sometimes.

It takes courage. Advocates need this in abundance.

The question then becomes: when is your judgement good and when is it bad?

It is never a mistake to consult other advocates not connected with your case. This is one of the greatest strengths of the robing room at court, and of being with other advocates in chambers or the office. So ask around.

ASK AROUND, d'you hear!

But be sure to explain all the relevant details. Another's opinion on only half the facts can be more than useless: it can be dangerous.

Having asked around, there will however occasionally still be times you are unpersuaded by everyone else, and you must still take the point.

Oh dear, you won't be liked.

In that case, you must **ENSURE YOU ARE RESPECTED**.

***

An advocate who is not respected is an advocate without credibility. Without credibility, we are unpersuasive.

The quickest way to lose respect is by being quarrelsome with the judge, or with the opposition, by taking mindlessly dull points which the robing room has sternly warned against, by being high-handed with witnesses, condescending to juries, pointed, irritated, arrogant, slightly sneering, and pompous.

Strangely, this really does happen.

Always guard against it. It can sneak up on you, unawares.

**

To maintain respect, it is only necessary to remember two things:

DEFERENCE to the judge and

POLITENESS at all times and to everyone.

Good manners are not weakness. Shakespeare said *manners maketh the man*. They are attractive and generally get you liked.

Deference is not weakness. In the face of heavy weather from a difficult tribunal, deference is the only way to proceed. There is no other route.

NEVER BECOME ANGRY WITH YOUR TRIBUNAL.

It may make you feel good, but you will lose.

You may think you have every justification, but you will lose.

If you fight your tribunal, someone must lose face. Unfortunately the tribunal will always have the power to decide who that should be—and it will always be you.

However with deference and politeness, no one need lose face, and it becomes so much easier to win the point, and so to turn slowly, slowly the enormous and seemingly unstoppable seatanker which is the tribunal's mind, if by doing so, no one is embarrassed. Turning seatankers is not easy—but it can be done. In court it is done with politeness, not with tub-thumping. If you tell a seatanker it is wrong, it will keep sailing at you, and as you are only a dinghy, you are in trouble, even if you are right. So always look for a way to make a point without making the tribunal lose face.

If you **SAVE THE FACE OF THE COURT**, you retain the respect of the court.

If you cannot be liked, make sure you are respected.

You will not be respected if you shout at the tribunal.

A respected advocate, although sometimes not popular, is a credible advocate.

And a credible advocate is a persuasive advocate.

A shouting advocate without respect is useless.

***

Another way of looking at guarding respect is this:

DEMONSTRATE YOUR COMPETENCE TO THE TRIBUNAL EARLY ON.

If you are thought competent early on, then you can even make some mistakes and not lose respect.

Find a way of demonstrating your competence.

Actively look for one.

Something easy.

And early on.

Show the tribunal you know what you are doing, with something uncontroversial. It might be timetabling for the case. It might be a list of the legal arguments that are to come. It might be correcting a spelling in the papers. Whatever it is, get some credit in the judicial bank with something helpful.

***

When you do open your mouth, **KEEP IT SIMPLE**.

***

Simplicity is more persuasive than big words, long sentences, multiple clauses, conditional subjunctives and other features of verbosity. This last sentence proves my point. It is too long.

Keep it simple. A simple sentence is short. It can be immediately understood. A tribunal cannot be persuaded unless it understands you. The most complicated cases, the most scholarly ideas, can generally all be reduced to simple sentences. All that is required is forethought.

Lawyers can be truly terrible for big words. It is as if we feel we must demonstrate all our professional expertise, all our learning, and just how clever we are, with a giant vocabulary.

We have spent years learning about things like *mens rea, actus reus*, maliciousness, recklessness, appropriation, subjective foresight, the balance of probabilities, and so the list goes on. These things are usually meaningless to juries and civilian witnesses. Avoid their use, except of course with the judge.

But even with the judge, only where necessary.

Find other ways of explaining what you mean as if sitting with new friends over a polite Sunday lunch.

***

Police officers often colour their language with odd stock phrases, designed perhaps to convey the impression their evidence is more measured, sounds more scientific, is more carefully researched, and therefore should perhaps carry more weight.

For example, they proceed in northerly directions on mobile patrols, instead of driving down the road; they disembark or alight from their vehicles, instead of getting out of their cars; they give chase and apprehend suspects, instead of running after people and catching them.

These expressions can sound dull.

They can confuse tribunals, and particularly juries.

So **TELL A STORY**.

Stories are not told with vehicles proceeding in northerly directions. Bring out the human dimension—the thrill of the chase, the struggle of the arrest, the speed of the cars, the shouting, the swearing, the excitement of finding a weapon—

To put it another way, **GIVE IT LIFE**.

***

And **BE BRIEF**.

***

We often feel we should keep talking to earn more money. Don't.

Don't pad out a submission or a speech or a cross-examination just to give the impression you are trying hard. You will be written off as a waffler.

Keep it simple. Give it life. Be brief.

**

At this point, we have the stuff of persuasiveness about us.

We are well dressed.

Our head is held up.

We do not hide.

We have control of our hands.

We move purposefully.

Our voice is a bit deeper and slower.

We have eye contact.

We stand like a rock.

At the optimum angle.

We are ourselves.

We do not try to be someone we are not.

We project our personality into the case.

We seek if possible to be liked.

At the very least we jealously guard respect.

We are polite to everyone.

Always.

We are deferential to the judge.

Always.

We check our judgment against the views of others.

We keep what we say simple.

We keep it brief.

We give it life.

And what we say should be **IRRESISTIBLE**.

***

It has been mentioned before, but it should be mentioned again.

IRRESISTIBILITY is the ideal point at which to conclude persuasiveness.

It is the hallmark of the truly great advocate.

An irresistible argument is just that—an argument which is irresistible.

The tribunal cannot fight it.

It sweeps them happily, effortlessly, to your conclusions.

No tribunal will accept a suggestion which is esoteric, contrived, or too clever by half, nor any idea which is thrust upon them.

***

To be irresistible, an argument is three things:

REASONABLE, not emotional,

SOFTLY DELIVERED, and

COMMON SENSE.

An irresistible argument is one which seems obvious, and is delivered in a manner which makes the advocate seem incidental, as if
almost not there. The cunning feature of the irresistible is it appears
no persuasion techniques are at work. Oh, but they are. They are
just hidden by careful word choice and skilful, measured delivery.

To be irresistible, there is no need to thump tables as if delivering
some fine 1930's oratory.

For all the law and rules of evidence we learn, for all the learning we
apply, the most persuasive feature of any case is if it accords with
common sense. If you can find the common sense position in any
argument, then you have the beginnings of something irresistible.
You then weave around the common sense position careful words
and a careful delivery.

Sometimes lawyers lose sight of common sense among all the books.
Don't. The winning argument is usually the easy argument. Sometimes, lawyers think things ought to be more complicated in order to
justify their years of learning. Some people actually look for the
more difficult argument. Don't. If it feels difficult, it is probably
wrong. The simple argument is often right, precisely because it is
simple, and if it is simple, it can be understood, and if it can be
understood, it can be persuasive.

So, **THE IRRESISTIBLE ARGUMENT IS USUALLY THE EASY,
SIMPLE ARGUMENT**.

Always ask yourself, what is the easy, simple argument? Where is
the common sense in this case?

How often have we read in the law reports in sometimes long and complicated cases the apparently simple and irresistible judgments of the great Lord Denning, and said to ourselves, "that's obvious, it's common sense".

The great thing about Lord Denning is how, through simplicity of expression and a healthy dose of common sense, he always looked obviously right, and it was only careful analysis by the House of Lords which could find flaws in his arguments. You want to be like him.

One can only imagine he must have been devastating, absolutely devastating, as an advocate.

***

Chapter VII

CASE PREPARATION

In crime, everything starts and ends with the charge.

The charge may be in a summons or a count on an indictment.

Before you do anything else, find out what the charge is.

As crime is my area of practice, we will proceed with preparing a criminal case. But in civil cases, the pleadings are central—before you do anything, read those.

Don't think for one second that the principles in this book do not apply to the courtroom in civil work.

You'd be way wrong.

So we'll work with crime. And I hope the civil people can join in.

***

A brief lands on your desk—thump. It is for the Crown Court.

Don't mess about with witness statements, unused material, correspondence, photos, instructions even. None of these things just yet.

GO STRAIGHT TO THE INDICTMENT.

It will tell you two things:

> **WHAT MUST BE PROVED** and
> **TO WHAT STANDARD**.

Usually the burden of what must be proved is on the prosecution.
Not always. Check the relevant statute. Trading standards prosecutions are examples of where the burden can lie partially on the
defence. Always be aware of the burden and standard of proof.

Always.

***

The following may sound crushingly obvious, but it is surprising how often advocates do not identify precisely what needs to be proved.

It can actually be useful to write it out.

If the allegation is assault occasioning actual bodily harm, the issues to prove are:

> Was there actual bodily harm?
> To whom?
> Was it caused by an assault?
> By whom?
> Was the assault unlawful?

Clearly there are more complicated variations on this theme for different offences, but the principle is a good one—**CLEARLY IDENTIFY THE ISSUES** as pleaded in the indictment or pleadings.

***

Once we know what has to be proved, we move to **HOW IT WILL BE PROVED**.

The answer is by the witnesses.

The case will be proved by the witnesses, not by the advocate. Obvious, but people often lose sight of this. The witnesses give the evidence which proves the indictment. The advocates will later argue over whether the witnesses have succeeded against the burden and standard of proof.

So now it's time to read the witness statements.

Not before.

Because now we know what the witnesses need to say to prove the issues, we read their statements to see if they do say it.

Again, it is surprising how often advocates simply never apply the evidence in the statements to each of the elements of the counts on the indictment.

Do the witnesses prove the counts? Look carefully at this.

Instantly we can now see every weakness—particularly if there is evidence missing. You will have identified case flaws if you're defending—if prosecuting, you need to produce an advice on obtaining further evidence.

But it is not only evidence which is missing that we notice. We also notice the sections in the witness statements on a crucial issue which are vague or unsatisfactory. We begin to sense where the lines of attack against the prosecution case will be easiest.

***

Now read all the papers.

Only now.

Read the proofs, and correspondence, and disclosed unused material, and so on. Reading it now means you can focus the material more clearly on the issues.

As a rule of thumb, in an ideal world, read all the case papers **THREE TIMES** before marking them.

There is no magic in the number, but at least you will really know the case now, and any marks on the papers will be geared toward a firm purpose, rather than idle under-linings of what later seems obviously irrelevant and mildly annoying if anyone else has to deal with the case.

***

Once you have read the indictment,
found what has to be proved,
looked up the law,
examined whether the witnesses prove what must be proved,
read all the papers three times,

Now
WRITE
THE
CLOSING
SPEECH.

That's right. Write the closing speech.

Do it now.

Not at the end of the trial. Not at the beginning of the trial. But now, way before even going to court.

Obviously, the precise words will change as the trial proceeds. But the purpose of **DOING THE CLOSING SPEECH WHEN YOU RECEIVE THE BRIEF** is it lights up precisely what you want from each witness.

Your closing speech is what you want to be able to say to the jury. It is a mixture of comment and reference to the evidence.

Once you know what you want to be able to say to the jury, you know what evidence you will seek from the witnesses.

Once you know what comments you want to be able to make to the jury at the end if the trial based on that evidence you will seek from the witnesses, it is

easy,
easy,
easy to work out precisely what you want from each witness.

So, in preparing the closing speech, you find the natural consequence is that instinctively you prepare your examination of the witnesses.

Whether you will actually get them to say what you want in the witness box is another matter for later discussion. But at least you now know what you would like them to say, and can gear your preparation toward thinking about exactly how you will get them to say it.

***

WRITE THE CLOSING SPEECH OUT.

Some people think this can be a simple mental exercise.

Not true.

Write out the points you want to make.

Succinctly.

Be bold.

Assume each witness will give you everything you seek: anger, inaccuracy, exaggeration, admissions of guilt, tears, agreement with whatever you suggest—whatever you want. Assume the best for your case, whether prosecuting or defending.

Ask yourself, in an ideal world, what comment could there be, what evidence would there be?

Write out the points.

Reflect on them.

Write them out again.

Delete a few as hopeless.

Add a few.

Write them out again.

How about doing it three times—again there is no magic in the number, but at least you now have a pretty clear idea of what you want to be saying to the jury, and what you want to hear from the witnesses.

Now prepare your examination of the witnesses.

Not before the closing speech has been written.

***

So what do we now know?

If prosecuting, we know what each witness must say to prove the charge, we know what comments we want to make in our speech; we can guess where the defence is most likely to attack. We therefore know now with what clarity, with what emphasis, with what anguish we wish the witnesses to give evidence of a material fact.

And if defending, we know what areas to cross-examine and we know what we want. Do we want the witness to appear a liar, or simply mistaken, or just likeably unreliable? We have identified who appears weak, where they appear weak, what answers most assist our case, what pieces of evidence to pluck from the statement and loudly emphasise, what pieces to deny, what pieces to avoid and if possible exclude.

With each witness, we have now identified a task. The task is— **ELICIT FROM EACH WITNESS ONLY WHAT YOU NEED FOR THE CLOSING SPEECH**.

Neither more nor less.

Hours of pointless examination and cross-examination have successfully been avoided, and our two advocates are honing like hawks straight onto the real issues.

***

Have you ever noticed how really able senior advocates actually look like hawks.

Eyes hooded,

Leaning slightly forward,

Head slightly bowed,

Each question focusing like a predator.

This is how you want to be, and you start by knowing precisely what you want to achieve during the case. And this means preparation. And preparation means doing your closing speech long before getting to court.

***

Remember, lawyers are always in danger of being very dull indeed, sometimes appearing to be creatures from another planet, never mind appearing to be hawks.

Juries are normal people. Lay magistrates are normal people. Sometimes we can find ourselves in an ivory tower and we forget what normal people think.

We get locked up in lawyerly machinations.

Don't.

BOUNCE YOUR IDEAS OFF NORMAL PEOPLE.

Ask your partner.

Ask your non-lawyer friends.

Do you think this argument in my closing speech is credible?

Do you think saying this in a speech works?

If the answer is no, find out why.

Welcome back to the real world.

**

The best advocates are those who know all the law, can do all the persuasive techniques, but for all that, they have not forgotten every lawyer's old favourite, the man on the Clapham omnibus.

Good jury advocates read The Sun.

No kidding.

They may not buy it, but they read it.

The paper is very much in tune with the way a lot of people think.

Keep in touch with the man who reads The Sun and sits on the Clapham omnibus.

And after you have bounced your ideas off your friends, where necessary, rewrite that closing speech.

＊

I've focused on the closing speech because it defines what you do during the trial.

Now I want to focus on preparing the examination of witnesses.

To do this, we have to understand the difference between **FACTS & COMMENTS**.

A witness gives a fact. An advocate makes a comment.

A fact is descriptive. A comment is prescriptive.

A fact is detail. A comment is argument.

An advocate needs a fact from a witness upon which to base his comment to the tribunal, as to why the fact means he should win the case.

No fact, then no comment.

So you want the fact to come out with just the right amount of colour and emphasis for the comment to be later attractive.

***

Let's look at an example.

You're prosecuting a burglar. It is a fact from the witness that there was an observation of the burglar at 10ft for 10 seconds in street lighting. The comment you want to make is the witness was therefore able to see the burglar clearly to be able to identify him, so that there has been no mistaken identification.

It is not enough to establish there was an observation at 10ft for 10 seconds in street lighting. You want more for the comment.

What date was it?—5 February.
What time was it?—6pm.
Was there any light?—there was street lighting.
Was there any natural light?—it was dusk.
How dark was it?—not that dark, getting dark.
Could you see?—yes.
Why?—there was street lighting and it was not yet that dark.
How far was the man you saw from the street lighting?—10ft.
Why do you say 10ft?—because I had a good look and I'm good at distances.
What colour was the street lighting?—orange.
What's your eyesight like?—I was wearing my glasses.
With glasses, what's your eyesight like?—very, very good.
How long did you see the man?—10 seconds.
How do you know it was 10 seconds?—I remember it was quite a long time.
How long is quite a long time?—at least 10 seconds.
Why 10 seconds?—it was long enough to take in everything about him and remember him.
What part of him could you see?—his whole body.
Could you see his upper half?—yes.
What of his upper half could you see?—his chest, his arms, his face.
How much of his face could you see?—all of it.
In what direction was he looking?—toward me.
What of his face could you see?—his eyes, his nose, his mouth, his hair.
What effect did the street lighting have on what you could see?—it helped me to see.

To see what?—his face.
How much of his face did the street lighting help to show?—all of it.

Your questions have teased out facts from the witness.

***

Now we have the perfect comment, based on the evidence we have
teased out, which has bolstered the simple observation of his face for
10 seconds at 10ft in street lighting:

> "It is respectfully suggested there is no mistaken identification.
> The distance was 10ft, over a period of 10 seconds. Let's count
> 10 seconds to remind ourselves of how that is ample time to see
> and remember a man's face. . . . . . Remember how the obser-
> vation was long enough for the witness with good eyesight while
> wearing glasses to observe, as he put it, everything about the
> burglar. Moreover, the street lighting was working, the witness
> has sufficiently clear recollection even to remember it was
> orange, and it must have been working well for the witness to
> tell us, not merely he saw the face, but to specify he saw the
> nose, mouth, eyes and hair. Think how delicate a feature is the
> nose—you wouldn't recall seeing that unless the lighting was
> good."

***

We work our comments around the evidence we elicit. We identify what evidence we need for the comment, with what colour, with what emphasis. Therefore, we elicit the evidence to make the later comment.

We identify what facts help us, and then we go get them from the witness. There is a symbiotic relationship, fact and comment revolving around each other. But remember, one is from the advocate, the other is from the witness, and the advocate only gets enough of the one to make the other—

He gets just enough of the right facts to make the later comment.

Don't ask the witness unnecessary questions.

Understand this.

If you don't comprehend the importance of avoiding unnecessary questions, ask around your colleagues. You need to really understand this, as the comment you propose to make governs everything you do in court. It governs just as much what you ask the witness, as what you don't ask.

Your closing speech, prepared long in advance of the trial, weaves the comment you want to make with the facts you want to hear.

***

Essentially, that closing speech is your **MAP**.

It tells you where you are going, what you have to do, where you have been, and where you have to get to.

It tells you everything you will want to do at trial.

***

So, from your closing speech, you identify the comment you want to make.

From the comment you want to make, you identify the facts you want to hear.

From the facts you want to hear, you identify the questions you want to ask and of whom.

It's that way round.

It is not,
not,
not,

NOT from what the witnesses say, you then identify what the facts are; and from what the facts are, you then identify what the comments are you want to make; and from the comments you want to make, you then craft your closing speech.

IT'S THE OTHER WAY ROUND!

***

Chapter VIII

ADDRESSING THE JUDGE

A judge is not a jury. A judge requires different treatment.

Contrary to some silly rumours, judges are usually wise, excellent lawyers, very experienced trial advocates, and fair.

Assume this to be the case.

In fact, it is usually a good idea to find out about your judge. Ask the usher what mood he is in. Ask in the robing room what he is like. Learning about your tribunal is part of your job. What you discover can be used to the advantage of your case, and can hone your address all the better to fit the judge's expectations.

***

Some advocates start with the belief the judge will be slow, other worldly perhaps, even daft: this is crazy advocacy. It annoys the judge and so you lose precious respect. It makes it more difficult to persuade the judge because now you are likely to be ignored, as it might be thought to be a loss of face for the judge to agree with you.

***

96   Chapter VIII

Understand the judge's need for formality. Don't fight it.

Judges occupy a formal position in society. They have enormous power within the law. They can separate families, they can change lives with jail sentences, they can imprison witnesses (and advocates) for contempt, and they can seize huge sums of money and freeze assets. Within society's pecking order, they are by necessity in a higher position in their court to all around them, and rightly so. Their important status is carried and made accessible by formality. There can be no other way. There should be no other way.

So a judge must be approached with

RESPECT and
DEFERENCE and
POLITENESS.

You can disagree, but always with deference.

You can agree, but always with politeness.

You may not see eye to eye.
But
never,
never,
never,
forget respect.

Ever.

He's in charge. You are not.

And if the judge senses you do not respect him, you will not be persuasive, which is your job, so you won't be doing your job properly.

***

Submissions should be **BRIEF**.

Nothing more needs to be said on this.

Remember it.

Full stop.

***

To a judge, a point need only be made **ONCE**.

Be sure however the point has been heard and understood.

EYE CONTACT will tell you if the judge has the point.

So too will the movement of the **JUDGE'S PEN**—watch the pen to see what is being written down, and do not race ahead of the speed of the pen when making your submission.

Don't keep repeating the same point as it does not get stronger by repetition.

Of course, what is permissible is to come at the same point from different angles—although arguably this is in fact making different points.

> *"The car was travelling too quickly,*
> *It certainly was not travelling slowly,*
> *It was speeding far above the speed limit,*
> *Travelling way too fast for the amount of traffic on the road."*

This all says pretty much the same thing, but in different ways. That's ok. But just don't keep repeating the car was speeding.

***

Your **OPENING PARAGRAPH SHOULD BE REHEARSED**.

It should capture neatly and succinctly the overall point you wish to make, and why. It should be a **CLEAR SUMMARY** of your position.

After your opening paragraph, provide the judge with a **STRUC-TURE** for the detail of your submission. List the areas you will cover. Allow him to write the areas down. Watch the pen.

Now take him to each area, and begin each area with a clear summary of it.

Then the detail.

Summary, then detail.

Remember that if the judge can follow your argument easily, this gives you respect and will help make you persuasive.

And what helps the judge to follow the argument is an opening clear summary. It provides a **MAP**. Judges love maps. With a map, they will understand where you are going and why. You become easier to understand. And if you are easier to understand, you may become dangerously close to being irresistible.

***

DO NOT ASSUME YOUR JUDGE KNOWS ALL THE LAW,

. . . OR EVEN ANY OF IT.

Remind him of it. Do not be afraid.

Slowly.

Refer to the authorities—slowly.

Read the relevant sections of statute—slowly.

Make sure your judge is on the same page, at the same paragraph, at the same word.

Pause, and allow the judge to arrive at the same point as you.

So many submissions are hurried, perhaps out of fear the judge will think he is being wrongly taught to "suck eggs", or perhaps out of simple nervousness.

But remember **JUDGES ARE PEOPLE, NOT MACHINES**. They cannot know everything in the law.

Sometimes a judge's recollection of a former case is just slightly inaccurate, in a material way which is highly relevant to your case. You won't know that unless you take him through the authorities—and you would not have known it if you have assumed he did not need to be reminded.

***

I've said earlier judges can be assumed to be excellent lawyers. Now I'm saying don't assume they know the law. Some may think I'm contradicting myself. I'm not. A judge cannot be assumed to know the letter of every statute and the precise ratio of every case. So much in a legal argument can turn on the precise words. What you can assume is that judges, as good lawyers, will be very able at absorbing the implications of the precise words. And they will usually thank you for reminding them. They will usually know quite a bit about the area under discussion. But it is best for the advocate to proceed on the assumption the area is new to the judge, and in this way, you will not make the mistake of assuming the judge knows a point of detail which in fact he does not, is then embarrassed you have assumed he does know it, and is now in danger of losing face, and so inclining against your argument to preserve his dignity.

Besides, the judge will often quickly point out the areas which are new to him. But from your point of view, it is best to assume it is all new, and in this way, you can't go wrong.

***

Judges sometimes like to have a **SKELETON ARGUMENT**.

This is particularly true of appeals and points of law.

They can be compulsory in civil cases and in the Court of Appeal.

If someone tells you a skeleton is a boring formality, they are wrong—skeletons can be a vital part of advocacy in a modern trial. They can put the judge on your side or against you before the case even begins. They are not a pleading. Instead, they are an opportunity to put your case in a good light and your opponent's in a bad one.

Different people say different things about skeletons. There is no right or wrong way to prepare them. What follows therefore is my own view.

A skeleton should be a **SHORT** document which lays out the **HEART** of the argument with references to the relevant law.

There is an art to these documents.

Both in how to prepare them and in how to use them.

***

A skeleton should whet the appetite—it should be a teaser.

Its purpose is to get the judge provisionally on your side.

What I suggest is that it should not be a treatise on every aspect of the argument.

It should not provide the judge with the opportunity to decide the issue on the strength of the skeleton. It should show the area where the argument is, and what you suggest is the answer, without being an exhaustive treatise on which the judge is offered the opportunity to disagree in the quiet of his room without you there.

Treatises may not be read fully. Moreover, what is there to say at the hearing if it has all been said in the treatise? And more to the point, you have no control over the judge while he is reading the skeleton before the hearing. If you have set out in the skeleton to persuade the judge, and the judge has been unpersuaded, you've lost, before you have opened your mouth, and yet it is when you open your mouth you should be at your most persuasive.

So don't set out in a skeleton to persuade. It should whet the appetite.

Hold something back.

**

The skeleton should provide a short summary of the facts as you would wish the court to find them, and a short summary of the law as you would suggest is how it stands, with clear references to where the law can be found, and briefly how you suggest the facts apply to the law.

No more than that.

Facts   —   as you suggest they are,
Law   —   as you suggest is relevant,
Then   —   how you suggest the facts fit the law.

Brevity, brevity, brevity.

The detail of the argument comes later, when you get to court.

***

There is a school supporting long skeletons. Some people suggest the skeleton should contain every aspect of the argument. It is fair to say this can work. It can be particularly effective in a Magistrates Court where there is a lay bench who may be impressed and even a little intimidated by a full argument, so that they believe you must be right if you have written so much.

However, on balance, my own view is that a long document risks the court having made its mind up before you get to argue the point. In time you will find your own style. I suggest you start short, and get longer if that suits you better.

***

So what do you do with the skeleton at court?

Use it as your map.

Don't read from it.

But do quote from it.

Begin your argument by capturing the bulls-eye point in a neat opening sentence.

Then identify what you say are the facts, pointing out where you have mentioned them in the skeleton.

Now develop where you say there is an argument with your opponent on the facts, and why you should win it.

Explain how you suggest the law fits the facts as you suggest they are. Identify where the arguments lie, and explain why your argument beats the other side, reminding the judge of what is in the skeleton.

Take your time.

***

Refer back to your skeleton time and again, quoting from it, and then delving into detailed argument. Anchor your judge to the skeleton, and then take him on a tour of the legal battlefield, bringing him back time and again to where you say the best vantage point is for considering the argument, which ought always to be in the skeleton. In this way, if you take him to where you say the best vantage point lies, you have an attractive opportunity to show him the legal battlefield from your point of view.

Think of a skeleton as a pair of binoculars with which Wellington surveyed the battlefield of Waterloo. Lend the judge your binoculars. Of themselves, they will not win the battle, but they can help.

Come to think of it, Wellington had a telescope—binoculars had not yet been invented in 1815. But you get the point.

***

When addressing a judge, remember to try to see the overall position from his point of view.

I have mentioned this before, but it is so important, I could mention it on every second page.

From the point of view of the judge, you are there to **ASSIST**. And a judge will value your assistance. He will want to understand your argument even if he will disagree with you in the end. Don't rush, don't hide, stand solidly, reassured by the knowledge that with politeness, deference, a slow delivery, one point at a time, assuming the law to be new to the judge, perhaps with a good, short skeleton, and above all with respect, just about every judge will listen courteously and with approval.

**

CHAPTER IX

THE OPENING SPEECH

This chapter is written with crime in mind, and I am conscious it may not translate effectively to civil practice. It presupposes your audience is a jury. Some ideas will translate and the reader is invited to pick and choose.

In crime, the opening speech will usually apply to prosecutors.

It is rare to make a defence opening speech, which is more of an art and very risky. Unless you are very experienced, *don't do it*. The principle problem is creating hostages to fortune, where you say to the jury they will hear certain evidence. By this stage in a trial, the jury really wants to know what the defence will be saying. If the defence witnesses don't say what you say they will say because they go off script, the jury can think it really significant and hugely hold it against your case.

So unless you know how to control witnesses, which you probably don't yet if you are reading this book, and unless you have developed that nose which tells you whether the witnesses really will tell you what they say in their prepared statements, which you probably haven't yet as it will take you about seven years of experience to develop that nose, just don't do it.

***

A prosecution opening speech before a jury should review
the facts,
the law, and
the burden and standard of proof.

The precise order is a matter for individuals.

Many find it makes sense to start with a short, simple opening paragraph, which completely, neatly and succinctly in a nutshell tells the court what the case is about. We can call this the **SUMMARY**.

Then it helps to explain the **BURDEN AND STANDARD OF PROOF**.

Now explain the **DETAILS** of the facts as it is anticipated they will unfold.

Finally, explain **THE LAW**.

***

Summary,
Burden and standard of proof,
Details of the anticipated facts,
The Law.

***

Be careful explaining the law.

GET IT RIGHT.

Law can be boring and can be clumsily done. It can confuse rather than illuminate.

Draw the jury's attention to the indictment, and go through the particulars of the offence. Explain how the anticipated facts fit the law.

Deal with the indictment **BRIEFLY** and leave the details of the full jury direction to the judge.

Make sure you watch a number of openings, and discover the tempo of the delivery and the extent to which the law is explained. It is not too much. It is not too little. It is just enough to explain what crucial facts the jury need to seek in the evidence. It is just enough to highlight on what areas the most attention must be paid when the witnesses are giving evidence.

Remember most criminal allegations are easily understood, even if the detail of the law is unknown to the jury. Crime tends to centre round clear ideas of dishonesty, violence and lust.

Always write out what you propose to say on the law—don't wing it, as you are guaranteed to stumble over words, helplessly recalling as you blunder along that there is a complexity of legal directions in previous authorities, and you will go beet-red as you sprout perspiration while feeling His Honour's eyes swivel disapprovingly onto you.

***

Indeed, it is recommended you
WRITE OUT THE WHOLE OPENING,
particularly the details of the facts.

No kidding.

Always.

Even for simple cases of shoplifting.

I still do.

***

By writing out everything, the summary, the details, and the law, you will deliver a faultless performance.

In your first act before the court, you will therefore appear commanding.

You will have respect. You have demonstrated your competence early.

You will therefore already appear persuasive.

In addition, the jury will clearly understand you. As everything will have been carefully weighed beforehand, there will be no stumbling over the opening, giving rise to confusion and puzzled frowns. The jury now fully understands, and knows what to look for in the evidence.

And note this: by writing everything out, you will immediately have identified what evidence is missing and what evidence is weak. So from your carefully crafted opening words, you have the opportunity to minimise the importance of the weak, and emphasise the importance of the strong.

But remember this:
WRITING IT OUT DOES NOT MEAN READING IT OUT.

Reading is dull, and if you are dull, you will not be persuasive. Nor will anyone listen to you, so the point of your opening will be lost. You will probably remember much of what you have written anyway. Make sure you look up at the jury and don't look down all the time at the piece of paper upon which you have written your opening.

***

The importance of a good opening is another one of those things which cannot be overstated. Just think abut how hard it is for a jury to absorb what a case is about. Advocates have had time to prepare, and have had papers to study. They have learned about the case through reading and the use of their eyes, which is how we mostly absorb information. But juries learn with their ears. Think about how hard this is. Listening is difficult. Attention span is short.

And remember the environment is unfamiliar—wigs, gowns, docks, ushers, imposing figures on the bench in colourful robes. It is easy to feel uncomfortable and distracted. Your job is to make the jury feel comfortable. And you can do this with a good opening.

A good opening gives the jury a **MAP** (there's that word again) of what the case will be about, it stops them feeling distracted, and helps them to look for the significant evidence when a witness speaks. It is vital, and they will thank you for it, by giving you their ear whenever you speak.

***

The question often arises just how far should we go in an opening to persuade the jury we should win.

In other words, should we colourlessly explain the facts as appear in the witness statements, or should we attempt to create an atmosphere and put some colour before the court.

Unless you are very experienced, **COLOURLESS IS BETTER THAN COLOURFUL**.

However, as an aside, closing speeches should be colourful. They are different. They are the moment of persuasion. They contain comment. We'll talk more about them later. But an opening should usually be comment-free, simply reciting the facts as it is anticipated they will unfold.

So, keep the following in mind as not a bad rule of thumb:

Colourless opening,
Colourful closing.

***

However, let's talk about colourful openings for a moment.

A colourful opening is often said to be *"Opening High"*.

OPENING HIGH is where you attempt to poison the mind of the jury against the defendant straight away.

That is what you do—poison their minds. Strong words. And of course, it can be met with a strong reaction. If done properly, the prosecution are way ahead of the defence. If done badly, the advocate is disliked by the jury.

Particularly if done transparently so that the jury feel they are being manipulated.

If done badly, the advocate loses just about all credibility. So it is a risky business.

Phrases must be carefully chosen for maximum impact, but **SUBTLY**.

A small amount of indignation, affront, even outrage is gently injected into the advocate's poise, tone, and gestures. This requires considerable skill, and can easily be overdone. It actually takes years to learn how to do it well.

In the US, just about everyone opens high all the time. There, it is expected. In England, it is not. Don't be inspired by the splendid tv series LA Law—am I showing my age?—it was in the 1980s, brilliant stuff, I watched it every week—it's great tv, it really is—rent the dvds—but it makes for lousy courtroom practice in London.

Look instead to the Central Criminal Court at the Old Bailey. This is the greatest place in Britain, perhaps in the world, for *quality* high openings. Some of the ablest prosecutors anywhere on the planet can be found here. Visit the Bailey. Sit in the public gallery. Watch them at work. Learn from them. It's free and it's fantastic.

***

A key danger of opening high is saying that certain evidence will definitely be given.

Civilian witnesses are generally not reliable. Whatever they have said in their statements, they do not necessarily say in evidence. They get confused. They forget things. And sometimes, events have been overstated in the statement, so that in evidence at court, they are milder.

It is dangerous to open high on what civilians are expected to say.

***

Police officers however can be word perfect, as they are allowed to follow their notebooks, and will therefore usually say exactly what is in their statements.

Doctors are usually the same, as they will have contemporaneous notes to follow.

In fact, word perfect evidence can usually apply to all experts. Generally, they will be able to refer to their reports and provide their evidence precisely as you read it in the papers.

Remember, if you open high on evidence which does not mater-ialise, you look foolish, lose respect, and it is easier now to lose the case.

So the key is to **KNOW FOR SURE WHAT WILL BE SAID**.

***

Reasons for opening high are probably restricted to either serious cases with expert and police evidence of crucial importance where you know exactly what will be said, and occasionally to serious cases, perhaps like fraud, which will probably be a bit dull without the injection of a little drama at the beginning.

In the dull cases scenario you balance the risk the evidence will not reach the height of the opening against the risk that without a little colour the jury will switch off, not follow the case, and acquit.

So, a general approach might be this:

OPEN HIGH WITH EXPERTS, DULL CASES, OR SERIOUS CASES.

If you open high on a non-serious case, like shoplifting, you may come across as a Victorian prude.

***

In all other cases, which will be mostly your work in your early years, and unless you are very experienced, **OPENING LOW** is best.

Just relate the facts as they appear likely to be, no frills, no excitement, and let the witnesses carry the drama.

It is safe, because you have lost no credibility if the witness fails to come up to proof. You can bend your closing speech (which will usually be of a very different colour to your opening) to the actual evidence given.

A low opening is dispassionate, clear and a bit colourless.

It is a summary of the facts, as the prosecution anticipates them.

It is not a summary of the arguments.

Where there are civilian witnesses, it is better to give the gist of their statements rather than the exact words within them, or they may surprise you and the court by saying differently.

Let the civilians flesh out the case.

***

An opening should be delivered **SLOWLY WITH PLENTY OF PAUSES**.

The jury is just settling into the case. It wants to understand clearly what the case is about. Like I said, remember how distracted a new jury will be, with the wigs and gowns, the court layout, the appearance of the defendant, and allowances must be made for their distraction.

Settle the jury in gently and firmly.

Be sure they understand what you say.

Don't rush in the excitement of starting.

Show command.

Keep it simple.

***

At the end of the opening, you want the jury to think three things:

"We think you are credible, likeable even, sensible, you personally, not just your case,"

—and—

"We understand what the case is about, how the evidence is supposed to fit together,"

—and most importantly—

"We understand what evidence to look for from the witnesses."

Now you have the jury thinking with you.

They see you as their guide.

They will follow you.

You are now ahead of the opposition.

***

CHAPTER X

WITNESSES

Advocates have a remarkable privilege.

They are allowed to ask highly personal questions of people in a public arena.

And people must answer them.

Few others have this privilege, apart from judges.

There is a danger advocates can march into people's lives, turn them completely upside down, and waltz out for a glass of wine.

The public sometimes perceives this is what advocates do.

For the advocate, it is just another day's work.

But for the witness, who often has not been questioned in court before, the experience may have been devastating, and never to be forgotten.

Do not become blasé—**REMEMBER THE IMPACT** you will have on others' lives.

***

WITNESSES ARE PEOPLE.

They are not objects.

They are not for picking over disdainfully like some laboratory specimen.

There are some truly awful advocates who treat witnesses appallingly.

Never,
ever
be like that.

***

ALWAYS BE POLITE.

ALWAYS.

Even to the witness who is the greatest enemy of your case.

Especially to that person.

Anger,
disdain,
and answering back,
are
always,
always
dangerous.

Disdain makes you look arrogant and so you lose respect.

Anger makes you look as if you are losing.

Answering back makes it seem you are too involved in your case.

Try to envisage you are above the fray, while keeping a measure of common sense.

Some advocates can play the disdainful card well. But they are very experienced. If you play it badly, you will usually lose the case. So in the early years, don't do it.

                                   ***

Witnesses are usually intimidated by the court and the formality of wigs and gowns.

If they are your witnesses, **PUT THEM AT EASE**.

Settle them slowly.

Ask easy questions to begin.

Be wary of asking civilians to state their home address in open court—this often unnecessary request can completely unsettle them. Is a public declaration of a home address necessary? Can it be written down? Think about this.

Ensure questions are simply phrased.

One question at a time.

Look at the witness.

Eye contact again.

Smile, even—it works wonders.

Invite them to keep their voice up.

Invite them to address the tribunal directly, especially on really important points.

***

Develop a **SYSTEM** with your witness.

Question. Answer. Question. Answer.

Encourage the feel of dialogue.

Get a rhythm going.

But pace the speed of the dialogue to meet the judge's pen.

Keep things slow and even and pleasant, and the witness will feel more comfortable.

Remember that every witness has a personality. Try to tease that personality out, or they may in their discomfort appear wooden and lifeless and will perhaps wrongly be less likely to be relied upon by the tribunal.

***

And finally, for all the brooding atmosphere of a court, for all the formality and strangeness of it, your witnesses have a story to tell.

They may feel in front of lawyers it is a story which must be told in some formal manner with big words.

Stop them.

Get them to **TELL THEIR STORY**,
easily,
in their own words,
without worrying about impressing all the supposedly clever lawyers.

***

CHAPTER XI

QUESTIONS

Questions should be **SHORT**.

Each question should seek one fact at a time.

Only one.

Each question should be one question, not multiples of questions rolled into one long sentence.

One question seeking one fact.

"What is the make of your car?"
"What colour is it?"
"Is there any damage to its front?"

Not,

"Tell us about your car, for example its make, its colour, whether it has any damage to its front?"

One question seeking one fact.

In examination in chief.

And cross-examination.

Both.

Always.

The big problem is that multiple questions create a list in the mind of the witness, who is probably ill at ease anyway, can't then remember the list and will answer only one or two aspects of what has been asked, and possibly wander off script.

If you ask long multiple questions, you will look clumsy, you will confuse the witness, and you will undermine the credibility of both of you.

***

KNOW THE QUESTION BEFORE YOU ASK IT.

Don't set off in the expectation you will know what you want to say, as yours may be a long and clumsy voyage.

Questions should not be proceeded with *"Urmm Ehhh"* Ask your colleagues whether you do this, as you are almost certain not to be aware of it. Video yourself and check there.

If you are a member of the Urmm Ehhh brigade, here's a hopefully helpful hint:—make yourself conscious of exhaling slightly and quietly before each question. This will definitely kill it off.

Another hint is to concentrate before each question on wriggling your toes. I've mentioned this before. It cannot be seen. And the effort involved in wriggling them occupies your mind so much that you forget to do the Urmm Ehhh thing.

***

Urmm Ehhh is a fill-in. It is noise designed to fill in the space between answer and next question. Usually we feel uncomfortable in silence, when everyone is waiting for what we will say, so we feel the need to fill that silence with noise.

DON'T BE EMBARRASSED BY SILENCE.

Relish it. Use it to create tension. Use it to create command. Don't hide from it. All eyes are focused on you for your next question. So let them focus on you—stand like a rock and relish your control.

***

The other fill-in is *"Right"* or *"OK"*.

Don't do it.

Advocates sometimes say Right or OK in response to each answer. Again, you are unlikely to be conscious of it, so ask your colleagues. Or check the video.

The problem with Right and OK, aside from being irritating like Urmm Ehhh, is that it also suggests you are approving of the witness, and that you are signalling the correct answers to the witness. This has the effect of undermining the witness's credibility, and of course yours, because it may look as if you are telling the witness what should be said.

It is difficult to control. But you must make yourself aware of it.

And there are no helpful hints as to how to stop it. Try the short exhale. Or the toes.

Whatever.

Just don't do it.

And don't say *"and"* at the beginning of every question—another fill-in—highly irritating.

***

What happens with fill-ins is that the tribunal begins to listen out for them, and stops listening to the substance of the evidence, smiling inwardly at every time you do it again, thinking you are a buffoon.

You can't be persuasive if they think you a buffoon.

Yet another fill-in is the repeated answer.

Advocates sometimes idly repeat the answer just given to fill in thinking space before the next question.

It is the most irritating thing you can do.

And it completely undermines your credibility as it makes you look as if you are over-emphasising the evidence.

With any luck, the judge will stop you.

However, do not confuse the *idle* repetition of the answer with **DELIBERATE REPETITION**.

A deliberate repetition is where you repeat an answer which has been really devastating against the opposition.

Repeat it slowly.

Let it hang in the air.

Look to the tribunal for good measure.

And only do it once or twice with a witness or you'll be written off as a drama freak.

***

CHAPTER XII

EXAMINATION IN CHIEF

Some say this is the most difficult skill.

In some jurisdictions it is called *direct* examination.

It is more difficult than cross-examination.

Why?

Because without leading the witness, we must extract the relevant evidence.

WITHOUT LEADING.

With police officers and experts, this can be easy since they can refer to their notes.

Civilian witnesses on the other hand rely on **MEMORY**.

Incidents can appear different to them months later, and often they will wander off the point and must be brought back to what is relevant.

A witness at ease, to whom you have smiled, and gently settled with clear opening questions, is more likely to say what you require.

Always remember, the mind of an uneasy witness is generally blank.

***

On matters in dispute, you cannot lead.

ON MATTERS IN DISPUTE.

There is nothing wrong with leading where matters are not in dispute.

ASK YOUR OPPONENT WHAT CAN BE LED.

Sometimes the answer is nothing.

But usually, things like the date, location, time of an incident, and the name and occupation of the witness can be led. By leading on these matters you can break the witness into the witness box gently, and settle them.

***

A leading question is one which suggests the answer.

It's a pretty simple concept.

However, the dividing line between leading and non-leading can be blurred.

Sometimes it can be as subtle as voice intonation.

Experience will ultimately tell you the difference.

The problem with leading is not simply that it can be objected to by the opposition. It is the reason it can be objected to you must understand.

If you lead, the tribunal knows you have suggested the answer, and so the value of the evidence is diminished.

Leading will undermine your own case.

***

As a rule of thumb, a non-leading question will begin:

WHO,
WHAT,
WHY,
WHEN,
WHERE,
HOW,
PLEASE DESCRIBE?

Questions which begin in this way are so non-leading, they can be called **OPEN QUESTIONS**.

***

But there are other types of non-leading question.

CLOSED QUESTIONS are questions which limit the witness's choice of answer. Remember, there must still be a choice, and that's the key to why they are non-leading. The choice has to be genuine.

Of course, while closed questions are non-leading, they can get dangerously close to leading.

There are two types of closed questions:

the word-choice,

—and—

the yes-no.

The word-choice closed question gives the witness a choice of words: was the man tall or short or average height? The word-choice offers a series of words to the witness which need to cover the whole range, and the court awaits which the witness will pick, namely tall or short or average.

The yes-no closed question invites the witness to answer yes or no: was the man tall? The choice is yes or no. This is very close to leading, but may not be, depending on how the evidence has developed. The danger is it may be thought you are suggesting the witness is tall.

***

So, be careful of asking closed questions without first having laid
FOUNDATION through open questions for the basis of your closed
question:

> Who were you with?—A man.
> Please describe the man—He was quite big.
> When you say quite big, was the man tall or short or average
> height?—He was taller than average.
> Was the man tall? Yes.

In the course of these questions, which are a mixture of different
types of non-leading questions, foundation is laid from the earlier
questions and the answers given, for the closed word-choice question
and then the final closed yes-no question.

**

With closed questions, **BE VERY CAREFUL OF VOICE INTONA-TION**. You may be accused of suggesting the correct choice of answer from how you ask the question.

***

With closed questions, **BE VERY CAREFUL TO PROVIDE A GENUINE CHOICE.**

I've mentioned it earlier, but it bears repeating.

If the answer you want is obvious among several choices, you will be criticised:

> Was it so dark you could not have seen anything, or were you able to see well enough to see the burglar's face?

In theory, there is a choice, but it is pretty obvious what you want the witness to say. The choice is not genuine. The question is leading.

On the other hand, the questions might be:

> What was the lighting like? (Open)
> —There was street lighting.
> Was it light or dark or dusk? (Closed word-choice)
> —It was dusk.
> What distance could you see? (Open)
> —10 metres.
> What could you see over that distance? (Open)
> —I could see the burglar.
> What of him could you see? (Open)
> —I could see his upper body.
> Could you see his head? (Closed yes-no)
> —Yes.
> What could you see of his head (Open)
> —I could see his face.
> Did you say you could see his face? (Closed yes-no—repetition for emphasis)
> —Yes.

If in doubt about whether a question might lead the witness, ask yourself what you would think if you were for the opposition.

***

Avoid the standard phrase: **WHAT HAPPENED NEXT**?

Sometimes the witness gives a marvellous answer.

Mostly however, the witness either gives too much detail, too little, or just plain wanders off the point.

***

To avoid losing control of the witness with *"what happened next?"* use instead **THE PIGGYBACK**.

The piggyback is a way of fixing the evidence in time or space, *by using part of the last answer in the next question*—note the italics in what follows:

Where were you?
        —I was on the sofa.
In which room were you *on the sofa*?
        —In the living room.
In the living room, what other furniture is there?
        —A table, a tv, another chair.
Could you see the *tv while on the sofa*?
        —Yes.
What of the tv could you see *while on the sofa*?
        —All of it.
While on the sofa, did you look at the *tv*?
        —Yes.
Did you notice anything about the *tv*?
        —Yes
What did you notice about the *tv*?

So far, no question suggests the answer.

For the answer to the question, please turn over.

***

"I saw a gun lying on top of it."

Ok, it's a bit mindlessly dramatic, but I'm trying to get you to remember piggybacking.

So remember it.

***

Take things **CHRONOLOGICALLY**.

It is easy to settle the witness if you start at the beginning, proceed to the middle, and go through to the end.

Surprisingly, there are many advocates who leap about the chronology. Also, witnesses often jump about backwards and forwards in time. Be aware of it, and stop it, lest the case becomes confusing.

However, if a witness misses some piece of evidence, let it go for the time being. Come back to it later.

Of course, this breaches the chronology rule.

But you will only rattle the witness if you keep asking what else was there?

And a rattled witness's mind goes even blanker.

In addition, you risk drawing the attention of the tribunal to your concern about missing evidence. The danger here is even if you do finally get the evidence, its value may be undermined if the tribunal feels your pleading and anxious repeated enquiry has prompted the witness.

But the really tricky thing is to remember to come back to it. It can be easy to forget.

***

Of paramount importance with any examination in chief is **KNOW YOUR OBJECTIVES** with each witness.

Your objectives will have been established while *writing the closing speech* on receipt of the brief.

Know what each witness needs to say for your case to succeed.

If you know precisely what you want, it is so much easier to get it.

And what you want is no more than is necessary for the closing speech.

Remember, examining a witness is not a general enquiry.

It is focused on what is needed for the closing speech.

And it is as short as it can be.

***

CHAPTER XIII

CROSS-EXAMINATION

The general rule here is **DON'T DO IT**.

People at law school dream of the day they will cross-examine. Their role model is rarely a real advocate whom they have watched in court. Usually it is a tv character, from LA Law, from Perry Mason, from Petrocelli, (I'm showing my age again?), from a host of bad films with bad plots, sometimes good films with good plots, and these role models are all **COMPLETELY USELESS**.

On tv, witnesses blub.

They are exposed as liars, cheats, villains.

They admit guilt.

They eventually agree tearfully with the cross-examining lawyer, the judge bangs his gavel, and there are gasps from the public gallery. The advocate swaggers to his seat while the witness seems meta-phorically a dead duck.

IT DOES NOT HAPPEN LIKE THAT IN REAL LIFE.

***

A witness under cross-examination does not want to agree with you.

He will fight tooth and nail to confound you.

He will misunderstand your questions.

He will provide evasive answers.

He will try to use your questions as an excuse to repeat the deadly features in his testimony which destroy your case.

But blub? Never.

"It's a fair cop guv', you've got me bang to rights?" Never.

Unlike tv, a witness has no script which must be followed. He will try everything to wriggle out from under your questions.

Every question in cross-examination is an **INVITATION TO DISASTER**.

It is an opportunity for the witness to hammer you and your case.

***

So your first thought is don't do it.

ASK YOURSELF IF YOU REALLY NEED TO CROSS-EXAMINE.

Some of us think we must ask everyone questions or we are not impressing the client.

Nonsense.

Obviously.

But it happens.

A lot.

Always start from the point of view: *if I can avoid it, I will.*

***

If you have to cross-examine, there are ten rules.

Ten.

For the first five years of practice, don't break them.

Ever.

Errr . . . you will, of course.

But you shouldn't.

You won't be able to help yourself. None of us can. But there are ten rules, and you should know them, backwards, and know when you are breaking them, every time.

If you are going to break a rule, you need to be asking yourself *"uh oh, I'm about to break a rule, should I, what is the advantage, will it go wrong?"*

The point is **YOU HAVE TO BE AWARE WHEN YOU ARE BREAKING THE RULES**.

In this way, you may not do as much damage as you would otherwise do if you did not know the rules and had no idea when, inevitably as we all do, you break them.

So, learn the rules.

Be able to say them in your sleep.

***

The first rule is **THINK COMMANDO**.

Don't lay siege.

Don't settle into each witness with books of questions.

Like a commando, *you go in, you get what you want, you get out.*

Remember, it's dangerous out there.

Every question invites disaster.

So
stealth,
cunning,
brevity,
should be your beacons.

It's a raid, not a siege.

***

The second rule follows from the first:

WHEN YOU HAVE GOT WHAT YOU WANT FOR YOUR CLOSING SPEECH,
STOP,
STOP,
STOP.

STOP.

D'you hear?

STOP.

Don't try and improve on answers.

Witnesses will sense you think you have them, and will back-track.

Weigh each answer against the closing speech you want to be able to make.

If the answer fits—
STOP!

And try not to say *"thank you"*, as it tips the witness off you have what you want, and they may start trying to undo what they have just said.

Just stop. Full stop.

***

The third rule is hard:

NEVER ASK A QUESTION TO WHICH YOU DO NOT ALREADY KNOW THE ANSWER.

Cross-examination should not be used to dig around.

You have no idea what you will find.

It may be helpful.

But watch out—it may not be.

At all.

And you are gambling your case.

Sometimes you have to gamble, but rarely please, and you must have the brain of a mathematical weasel, cunningly calculating the odds of a helpful answer from your experience of people and from your assessment of the personality of the witness.

And you won't have the courtroom dexterity of a weasel for several years.

***

What then is the point of only asking questions to which the answer is known?

The point is to **DRAW ATTENTION** to your case.

The jury will not yet have seen the witness from your perspective. So make them.

The witness says the burglar was Tommy Smith who he knows locally. Let us suppose the following facts have all appeared either in the witness statement or the evidence in chief (so you do not breach the third rule), but are peppered about all over the place. Your job is to draw the facts together to present a fresh perspective.

Your perspective.

It was 3am?	Yes
It was night-time?	Yes
The burglar was in the garden?	Yes
You were in the home?	Yes
You switched on the lights?	Yes
You saw the burglar?	Oh Yes
In the back garden?	Yes
40ft away?	Yes
At the front of the house there is street lighting?	Yes
He ran down the back garden?	Yes
Away from the house?	Yes
He climbed over the fence?	Yes
The garden is 50ft long?	Yes
He took 10 seconds to reach the fence?	Yes, about that
He took 5 seconds to clear the fence?	Yep
He was in a hurry?	Yes
You couldn't quite believe what you were seeing?	Yes
You had just woken up?	Yes
You were puzzled by a noise you'd heard?	That's right
You turned on the light?	Yes

You looked out the window?	Yes
You say he looked up at you?	Yes
And then he was off?	That's right

Let's say the issue is identification; and it should now be obvious what will be said in the closing speech.

If it isn't, you'll get some idea a few pages on.

Note how the questions, which are really a series of statements, have bent the perception of the case.

Cross-examination is all about **BENDING PERCEPTION**.

It's about getting the tribunal to begin to see the case from your point of view.

It is not about getting the witness to blub.

***

The fourth rule is demonstrated in the questions you have just read above:

ALWAYS ASK LEADING QUESTIONS.

Always.

Never ask an open question.

Tell the witness what the answer is you expect.

You should know what the answer ought to be since it will have been in the witness statement or evidence in chief or is abundant common sense, and so the witness ought to agree with your leading question.

A leading question controls the answer.

This is because:

**A LEADING QUESTION GIVES THE ANSWER,
AND THE WITNESS SHOULD SIMPLY SAY "YES".**

If you give the answer, you control the answer.

Controlling the answer means controlling the witness.

Cross-examined witnesses, out of control, are deadly.

Deadly.

You say what the answer is, and ask
"isn't that so?", or
"that's right, isn't it?",
turning a statement into a question.

Sometimes you don't even have to say the *"isn't that so?"* bit, as it is plainly understood that you are asking a question.

You don't ask—

> *"Did the cat sit on the mat?"*
>   —nor—
> *"Where was the cat?"*

You ask instead

"The cat sat on the mat, that's right isn't it?"

And because you know the answer from what is in the witness statement or from the evidence in chief, the witness will probably say "yes", no more than that, and is safely under control.

***

The very best way to lose control, so that the witness becomes deadly, is to ask for explanations.

***

The fifth rule then is

NEVER
EVER,
EVER,
ASK THE WITNESS TO EXPLAIN.

EVER!

This is also known as never ask the witness *"why?"*

The problem with an explanation from the witness is it will destroy an explanation from you. Your explanation is what you give in the closing speech. Asking a witness to explain will undermine the explanations you will want to give in that closing speech.

Witnesses will almost
always,
always
find ways of explaining, despite the most cunning plans of the cleverest minds.

It is not like in the films where they shrug their shoulders and admit they can't explain.

You may think there cannot possibly be an explanation, and so you perorate with the witness, delivering what you think is the killer blow. The witness is now fighting for his life. So, watch out—he'll come up with something.

And when he does explain, he will use it as an opportunity to take centre stage in court again, and persuade the jury of his testimony.

Persuasion is your job—do not let it be taken from you and taken over by the opposition.

***

The sixth rule flows inexorably from the fifth, and is so important that it is monumental, huge, just plain massive:

RESERVE YOUR COMMENT FOR THE JURY,
NEVER
EVER,
EVER,
EVER,
FOR THE WITNESS.

Sometimes this is known as do not ask *"conclusionary questions"*— these are questions which demand a conclusion from the witness.

In a roundabout way, we are avoiding asking for an explanation, which is the fifth rule. If you put a conclusion to a witness—if you put what will be your comment to the jury—what you are in fact doing is asking the witness to explain whether your comment or conclusion is correct.

Let's look again at our burglar.

From the evidence a few pages earlier, we will want to make the following comment to the jury:

"It was dark, he was 40ft away, he looked up, there was street lighting on the other side of the house, but no evidence of lighting in the garden, he shot off, he was in view 15 seconds, but the witness must always have been looking at his back as he ran away, if the face was visible at all it cannot have been more than a fleeting glance of someone speeding into darkness, he had just been roused, had been fast asleep, was puzzled, couldn't believe his eyes, looking out a window which because it was night time with a light on in the room as a matter of common sense will have largely reflected the witness and the bedroom obscuring his view out. So in all, we have what must have been a glimpse in darkness over a distance of 40ft from a disconcerted sleepy homeowner which is not enough to make an independent tribunal sure of the identification."

Great comment.

But how often do advocates call for a conclusion from the witness.

Here's the stupid question—and believe it happens all the time: *"In all these circumstances I have asked you about, you did not see him long enough or clearly enough to make an identification about which you can be sure, can you?"*

And the reply?

***

"Of course I did. I have 20–20 vision, and he looked up at me,
for longer than a glance. You had not asked before for how
long he looked at me—it must have been 10 seconds. I could
see he was thinking what he should do. The bedroom light lit
him up clearly. And I was wide-awake, having been frightened,
not just puzzled by the noise. Oh, it was Tommy Smith all right.
He knew I'd recognised him. I could see it in his face. That's
why I guess he paused for so long before running off. Our eyes
met. It was him."

Oh dear. You have spectacularly lost control.

What was looking attractive has been undone by being over-eager to
get the witness, LA Law style, to crack up.

So just don't do it.

Never ask why.

Never ask for an explanation.

Reserve your comment for the jury.

                         ***

The seventh rule is:

NEVER ASK THE WITNESS FOR HELP.

A witness under cross-examination will kick you in the head—and that is what asking for help invites. It exposes your neck and invites decapitation. You will get no pity from the witness: he will have you.

Help problems usually arise after breaking the third rule about always asking questions to which you know the answer, or breaking the fifth rule about never asking for an explanation. Having asked questions to which you don't know the answer, you will usually have accumulated a series of crippling answers, and maybe an explanation which devastates you, and so you are off-balance, drowning before the jury.

So, with a meek smile, as you go down for the last time, you ask for a life belt:

"Surely you cannot be certain of the identification, I mean it really was dark, that's fair isn't it?"

(and we can almost hear a plaintive *"please say you agree, please help"*).

There is no life belt, simply the concentrated rattle of evidential machine gun fire from your implacable enemy, the witness, straight between the eyes and you sink without trace.

***

Instead, learn to look unconcerned by devastating answers. It's an act, but it is one you must learn. With a devastating answer, a tribunal will look to you, rather like an audience at a tennis match following the ball as it is belted back to you, and you must look like you can handle it. If you look as if the ball has got past you, the tribunal will take note.

Just say:

> "*I dare say. . .*" or
> "*Oh, I see. . .*" or
> "*That's helpful. . .*"

Make it look like everything is fine.

Whatever—just don't look like you need help.

***

The eighth rule is:

ASK ONLY ONE THING AT A TIME.

Some advocates roll large amounts of material into a question. In the confusion created by asking too much, the witness does not answer yes or no, but sets out once more on a lengthy explanation.

Lengthy explanations will destroy you.

They allow the witness to re-assert control

Importantly, they tend to allow the witness to repeat his story.

If the tribunal hears the story once, they might believe it. If twice, they're pretty much convinced now. If you blunder into allowing a third story-telling, nothing short of nuclear war is likely to change the tribunal's mind.

So, none of this:

"It was dark, being night time, with street lighting to the front of the house, and you looking out the window into the back garden, isn't that right?"

One thing at a time:

It was dark?	yes
It was night-time?	yes
The street lighting was at the front of the house?	yes
You looked out the window?	yes
At the back of the house?	yes

***

The ninth rule is:

WHEN PUTTING YOUR CASE, TELL THE WITNESS HE DIS-AGREES WITH IT.

This may sound weird.

But it is important.

Generally in England, we must put our case to the witness. In some other jurisdictions, you may not have to.

How much of your case to put, and in what detail, can depend on the individual case. There is an art to it, which you will learn with experience, and is not susceptible to written rules in an advocacy book. The general approach is to put as little as is necessary to have fulfilled your duty to have put it.

The reason advocates are wary of putting their case in glorious technicolour is this: if you're not careful, putting your case can become an opportunity for the witness to take centre stage to say at length exactly why your case is wrong and should be disbelieved.

The witness will repeat the best points in his evidence, will add a few more, and will look keenly at the jury persuading them to believe him.

So, don't ask: "*I suggest your identification is mistaken, what do you say about that?*"

You'll get a very long answer.

Instead, how about: "*I suggest your identification is mistaken, but you would disagree with me, wouldn't you?*"

The answer is "*yes*".

And only yes.

You have not invited justification from the witness by challenging him to an evidential fight to the death.

You have instead asked a question which invites **AGREEMENT** from the witness, namely *"Yes, I disagree"*.

The answer is neutral, uneventful, perfectly agreeable, and everyone has expected it anyway. You have done your duty in putting your case and you have avoided a diatribe in response.

***

The tenth rule concerns **BOUNCE FOR CONFRONTATIONS**.

Bounce is again about bending perception.

We mentioned bending perception at the end of the third rule.

Bounce is supremely important.

How do you get a witness to say what you want?

In an ideal world, you want the witness to cry buckets and confess their lies, to say *"It's a fair cop guv', you've got me bang to rights, I've been lying"*. They never do.

But the question is, can you get close to it?

Can you create the **IMPRESSION** it is a fair cop, the witness is bang to rights, but naturally and understandably, he cannot bring himself to admit it?

Bounce is required.

***

You bounce your case off the witness.

Imagine a tennis ball being thrown at the witness, to bounce off the witness, into the hands of the jury.

We use bounce only when we confront a witness.

Unlike our identification witness who we say is simply honestly mistaken and against whom there is no need to bounce, we use bounce if suggesting a witness is the wrong-doer, the guilty party, the real culprit, the wrong'un.

For example it is highly effective where the allegation is assault and the defence is self-defence.

You put your case in great detail, simply bouncing it off the witness to the tribunal.

Get a rhythm going.

The psychology of what you are doing should mean it appears irrelevant to the mind of the tribunal what the witness says in response.

You say he hit you first	—Yes
But you hit him first	—No
You say he hit you on the nose	—Yes
But you hit him on the shoulder	—No
First	—No
With a pool cue	—No
While angry	—No
Because he'd looked at your girlfriend	—Not true
In a funny way	—No
So you hit him	—That's a lie
With a pool cue	—No
Twice	—Not true
And he hit you	—He did hit me
On the nose	—Yes
In self-defence	—No it wasn't

Notice how none of the questions in the bounce cross-examination
have question marks after them. You are not asking. You are not
seeking agreement. You are telling him, and expect disagreement.

***

And while delivering the bounce, do not look at the witness.

LOOK STRAIGHT AHEAD,
into space,
or at the judge,
or occasionally for emphasis to the jury.

This is the moment you clash swords with the witness.

This is not forensic surgery: it is forensic war.

Polite war.

Remember what we said about always respecting the witness.
CROSS-EXAMINATION IS NOT "CROSS" EXAMINATION.

And if you come off badly from clashing with the witness, at least
you have been polite, so you have not lost too much precious
credibility with the tribunal. But you will if you are rude and then
lose. Tribunals hate rudeness. Rightly so. You don't know what
really happened in a case. You are simply following instructions. So
when you bounce, be formal, be firm, but **DON'T GET PERSONAL**.

And use your stature, your head held high, your body movements
purposeful, your deep voice, your politeness, your short questions, as
you bounce to persuade the jury your case is right and the witness is
wrong.

***

Remember, the witness has less armour in the witness box. You have a robe, maybe a wig. You are protected by books and files. You are practised at persuasion. You have done it before. You have an advantage.

Use it.

You'll often look more of an expert than the witness on the witness's own case.

Wield that sword.

But always politely.

***

I wish now to speak of something I call "the lever".

When considering bounce, we may look for THE LEVER—it is notionally what drops the witness through the evidential trapdoor when pulled.

But be careful. It can be upsetting in court and should only be reserved for the "right" witnesses. We can look for it in every witness, whether using bounce or not, and we must always ask whether it should be pulled.

Sometimes to pull it unsettles the tribunal. To take an obvious example, it need not be done where a mother is giving character evidence for her son. You don't need to put it to her that she is simply helping one she raised, nursed, helplessly loves, and is incapable of telling the truth knowing her boy will go to jail. You might carefully make that comment later, but Mum does not deserve harm for showing loyalty. A tribunal will sometimes find that loyalty agreeable, while it will nevertheless politely disregard the testimony.

So remember—a tribunal will be unhappy if you pull the lever on the "wrong" witness.

***

For almost any witness there is some feature of evidence which is just not quite right. It leaves him open to attack, to being undermined, or to mild embarrassment. I don't mean exclusively stinging, red-faced embarrassment. I mean the sort that creates a moment of silence and everyone realises something is wrong; like when a fisherman tells tales of how big was the fish, or when someone overstates how good they are at speaking French, but then cannot follow what you say in the language. It is the embarrassment which follows when you catch someone out, and is the most effective result of cross-examination. If you destroy a witness, sometimes he receives sympathy. But if you embarrass a witness, the moment can hang like lead.

So, the lever should create embarrassment.

The thinking is: *if I pull this, does the witness get written off?*

Or: *if I pull this thread, does the testimony unravel?*

***

There is another way to think of the lever.

My Head of Chambers, the late great Michael Hill QC, used to speak of fishing and getting a nibble. You have to know when an evidential fish is near the line, unknowing but moving the hook, and how suddenly you then strike. It takes instinct and experience.

I can't teach you much about it, other than to keep your eye out for the day you understand my meaning. While I can teach you how to play the advocacy *Fur Elise*, perhaps note-perfect and a tad wooden, creditable nonetheless, I cannot teach you how to *feel* the music—but it will come.

***

A frequent example of a lever is a previous inconsistent statement. This is where a witness has said something in evidence which can be contradicted by referring to what is accurately recorded as having been said by him previously.

It sounds easy to do, but there is a method.

If not followed, you will probably go wrong.

***

The first step is to refer to the evidence in chief. Get the witness to repeat what he said.

Let's suppose he earlier said: *the cat sat on the mat.*

Your question is: *"It is right, is it, that the cat sat on the mat?* The witness will **CONFIRM**. If necessary, use the judge's note or your own to pin the witness to extract the confirmation.

***

Now you box the witness in by making sure there is no room for manoeuvre. We call this **RINGFENCING**, locking off escape routes. This is the most important part of the exercise.

> *You mean the black cat, not some other cat?*
> *You mean on Monday, not on Tuesday?*
> *You mean the mat in the frontroom, not the bedroom?*
> *You mean in the morning, not in the evening?*

Now you give the witness plenty of evidential rope to place around his neck. You point out the importance of the witness being right that the black cat sat on the mat in the living room on Monday morning. Tell the witness if he has made a mistake, he should say so. Assuming the witness does not back out, and at this point undermine himself anyway, the witness is perfectly poised on the evidential gallows.

***

Now you turn to the document which is the previous inconsistent statement.

First, you get the **ORIGINAL** document.

Then you pass it to the witness to agree its **AUTHENTICITY**, drawing his attention to his signature upon it, or some other feature of reliability, and at the same time being careful to stop him reading it.

A formal statement will often include a signed **DECLARATION** that it is true to the best of his knowledge and belief and he is liable to prosecution if he says anything he knows to be false or does not believe to be true.

Then you draw attention to **WHY ITS CONTENTS MUST BE TRUE.** You turn to why he made the statement. Draw out how he knew it to be important, perhaps that it was made to a police officer, and that as a record he appreciated it might be used in court proceedings.

Here is what you say:

> *"Here is an original document—it is your statement to the police, which you know to be an important matter—please note that your signature appears upon it under the declaration of the truth of this statement, your having reviewed this statement before signing so important a declaration, that's right is it not?"*

(Read out the declaration)

***

Now, take the witness to the relevant section which contradicts his testimony and **READ IT OUT**—don't ask the witness to read it out—you do it, or the witness will slip away, pretend not to be able to read, will have forgotten his glasses, will start form the wrong section, will read only that which embarrasses your case, and will take over the pace of the cross-examination—no, you read the section, asking him to follow.

Here is what you say:

> *"On page three, in the second paragraph, on the third line, we see a sentence which starts 'I was in the frontroom. . . ', do you have it?*

(Pause while the witness catches up).

> *"Please correct me if I read this incorrectly. Your statement reads: 'I was in the living room on Monday morning. I have a cat. It is black. The cat likes to sit on a mat in the living room, only that morning, the cat was nowhere to be found.'"*

(Pause)

(Look to the tribunal)

***

Now pull the lever.

> *"In evidence you say the cat sat on the mat, in the statement you signed as true you say the cat was not around—which is the lie?"*

You drive an unanswerable rhetorical **WEDGE** between the answers. This is pure bounce—it won't much matter what the witness says.

Obviously, the lever on previous inconsistent statements is the bread and butter of cross-examining defendants, whose police interviews are often full of inconsistencies.

Learn to do it well—it is a critical feature of effective cross-examination.

***

The key concepts to using a previous inconsistent statement are:

> **C**onfirm the evidence in chief,
> then **R**ingfence,
> produce the **O**riginal,
> confirm **A**uthenticity,
> refer to the **D**eclaration,
> and **W**hy the statement is true,
> **R**ead out the inconsistent section,
> then drive a **W**edge.

Taking the first letters of the key words *confirm, ringfence, original, authenticity, declaration, why, read* and *wedge*, we have CROAD-WRW and we can create a mnemonic sentence:

> ***Carefully ringfence, or a dodgy witness runs west.***

If you follow the meaning of the mnemonic, and the meaning of each of the first letters, most cross-examinations on inconsistent statements will work remarkably well.

***

Let us summarise what we have learnt.

Please remember—Don't cross-examine unless you really have to.

But if you have to, here are the ten rules again.

THE TEN TOTALLY TREMENDOUS RULES OF CROSS-EXAMINATION

1.   Think commando.

2.   When you have got what you want for your closing speech, stop, stop, stop.

3.   Never ask a question to which you do not already know the answer.

4.   Always ask leading questions.

5.   Never ever, ever ask the witness to explain—never ask *"why"*.

6.   Reserve your comment for the jury, never ever, ever for the witness.

7.   Never ask the witness for help.

8.   Ask only one thing at a time.

9.   When putting your case, tell the witness he disagrees with it.

10. Remember bounce for confrontations.

Look for the lever, but only use it for the "right" witness.

And when using a previous inconsistent statement, always remember *"carefully ringfence, or a dodgy witness runs west"*.

***

CHAPTER XIV

RE-EXAMINATION

In general, **DON'T DO IT**.

Only do it if you are very good.

It tends to highlight to the tribunal the areas you think are weakest in your witness.

And if you don't do it, it often makes it look as if you feel your witness has done well, even when he hasn't.

***

One circumstance for re-examination is where cross-examination has opened up an area for exploration which you would not have been allowed to explore in examination in chief. But the point here is this is not truly re-examination—it is more a species of examination in chief you are allowed after cross-examination. True re-examination goes over ground covered in chief which was then battered under cross.

An example of a new area might be in a domestic violence case where under cross-examination there are questions about the history of violence in a relationship which you could not have asked in chief as the evidence had been limited to the allegation on the indictment. Arising from the cross-examination, you may be able to ask the witness to go through the whole history. You would need the permission of the judge. But as you can see, it is a species of renewed examination in chief—it is about teasing out new material.

***

A particularly good reason for re-examination is **TO MASSACRE** your opponent.

If the witness is twitching with righteous indignation at a bad cross-examination by the opposition, let him repeat the core points of his evidence, ask him if he agrees with the foul suggestions made by the opposition, ask him if he is inaccurate or exaggerating, or unreliable, or lying, whatever, and finish with the question:

"Finally, is there any truth in the suggestions made by my learned friend?"

You massacre your opponent's case.

You massacre his credibility.

***

CHAPTER XV

IMPROVING QUESTIONING

There is a drill which can work wonders at improving your ability to ask leading and non-leading questions.

It will teach you the difference between them.

It will teach you to be comfortable with the difference.

To improve non-leading technique you need two colleagues, three pieces of paper and three pens.

We'll call them Jack and Jill.

Jill draws a simple shape which you do not see.

With your pen in hand, you ask questions of Jill to describe her drawing.

You now draw what you hear described.

And Jack does the same. He draws what he hears described by your questions of Jill.

Both of you, separately, without helping each other must draw **EXACTLY THE SAME SHAPE AS JILL**: same angles, same size, same scale.

***

Exactly the same.

Your questions must be precise to elicit the precise location of the various lines in the shape.

> What shape have you drawn?
> *A boat*
> Has it sails or funnels?
> *Funnels*
> How many funnels?
> *Two*
> How many decks?
> *Two*
> Is there smoke rising from the funnels?
> *Yes*
> From both?
> *Yes*

And so on

At the end of the exercise, compare drawings. Check your drawing with Jill. Check Jack's drawing with Jill.

The more exactly your drawing matches hers, the more accurate and focused your questioning has been.

And because you have not known what her shape was, your questions will naturally have been non-leading.

***

And here's the clever bit. The more exactly Jack's drawing matches Jill's, the more effective your questions have been to the ear of an audience.

A tribunal is an audience.

In other words, you will get some idea of whether, from your questions, a tribunal could have formed the **SAME MENTAL PICTURE** as you have formed and as has been formed in the mind of Jill.

This exercise allows you to measure how effective your questioning is.

***

Now for leading questions.

To improve leading technique, you need Jack and Jill, two pieces of paper and two pens.

Jack draws a shape unseen by Jill.

You look at Jack's drawing and you ask leading questions of him.

Through the leading questions you describe the shape.

Jill listens to the description you put to Jack.

If your leading questions are unfocused or clumsy, Jack will disagree with what you put to him, just as a real witness would under cross-examination.

You want Jack always to answer yes. This is the key to leading question technique.

But you want to be so methodical and focused in the questions that they basically amount to instructions to Jill about how to draw exactly the same shape.

> The shape is a boat?
> *Yes*
> It has 2 funnels?
> *Yes*
> Each funnel produces smoke?
> *Yes*
> The boat has one deck?
> *Yes*
> The bow of the boat is one inch from the left edge?
> *Yes*
> The rear of the boat is two inches from the right edge?
> *Yes*

And so on.

***

At the end of the exercise, look at Jill's drawing.

It is a representation of the picture you have created in Jill's mind.

Once again, you can measure the effectiveness of your questioning as you now have some idea of the sort of picture you have created in a tribunal's mind.

* * *

These exercises work.

Very well.

Try them.

Often.

The learning curve is exponential.

***

CHAPTER XVI

THE CLOSING SPEECH

The closing speech is the reason advocates exist.

It is their weapon, their art, the moment for persuasion.

Some say the advocate's greatest weapon is cross-examination.

Not so.

A good speech can recover a bad cross-examination.

But a bad speech can lose an otherwise winnable case, even after a good cross-examination, especially if your opponent makes a good closing speech.

***

Remember how everything throughout the case should have been geared toward the closing speech.

The speech should have been sketched out on receipt of the brief.

All the evidence elicited should be weighed against how it will affect closing.

Questions of witnesses will have stopped short of comment: just enough evidence will have been elicited to allow comment later in the closing.

Closing is when you draw together all of the case, all the answers from the witnesses, all the little incidents which arose at trial, and you present your theory of the case.

The speech you make in court ought to be within 80% of the speech you sketched on receipt of the brief: if so, you have run the trial well; if not, something has gone wrong.

**

Closing it is all about persuasion.

100% persuasion.

This means 100% comment.

It is not about the facts: it is about comment on the facts.

It is not about *repeating* what the facts were: it is about *explaining* why the facts as they emerged in trial mean you win.

*＊＊＊

The very first thing to say about a persuasive closing speech is this:

ALWAYS WRITE IT OUT.

At the very least create a fairly detailed note.

Always.

Absolutely always.

Do not try to wing it.

Do not assume you will be inspired as you open your mouth, and that words and ideas will flow, and the case will come stunningly together.

You will be wrong.

You will miss points.

You will express good points clumsily.

You will blunder into points which are very much against you, flapping for some means of minimising them, instead of nimbly, deftly, subtly, and with **MEASURED FORETHOUGHT** skirting around them.

Write it out.

Not necessarily every word, but **CONSIDER EVERY SENTENCE** you will utter.

Arm yourself with careful phrases which powerfully capture your case.

***

If you need time to write out the speech and draw together the best points, **ASK FOR TIME**.

Do not be afraid to do so.

It often happens in Magistrates Courts or County Courts, where the pace of hearings can suddenly mean the time has come to make your closing speech.

Ask for time.

This is your moment—your client's moment through you.

Don't let it slip through your fingers.

In a Magistrates Court, you should only need five minutes to gather your thoughts—but get those five minutes.

***

I mentioned something earlier which needs repeating, and elabora-
tion, and on your part, memorisation.

The whole point of a closing speech is to **TELL THE TRIBUNAL
WHY YOU WIN**.

When preparing your closing speech, your first line *inside your head*
ought to be:

"We win because. . ."

There may be several "we win because. . ." sentences. Having
identified them, now develop them.

Closing is not a description of the evidence. It is not a summary of
the evidence. It is a series of comments on the evidence. It is
argument, not regurgitation.

Let's say that again: **IT IS ARGUMENT, NOT REGURGITATION**.

It draws on the evidence which has been heard and explains to the
tribunal by reminding it of the evidence why the evidence means you
win.

Do not simply repeat the evidence.

Don't simply say: *"it was dark and the burglar was 40ft away."*

You do it this way: *"it was dark and therefore the witness may be
mistaken, can you be sure she is not? Moreover, in that darkness, you
are asked to be sure the witness is not mistaken when peering into a
distance of 40ft. It is my respectful submission that such a distance in
such darkness makes you understandably hesitate before you can say
you are sure there was no mistake."*

When you weigh a fact, ask yourself, *"why does this fact mean I
should win?"*

Don't assume anyone will guess why you win—spell it out.

Every time, spell it out.

***

"Three" is an important number in speeches.

When dealing with a jury, (not a judge!), it is usually a good idea to:

TELL THEM WHAT YOU WILL SAY, then
TELL THEM IT, and then
TELL THEM WHAT YOU'VE SAID.

In this way, you repeat your best points three times.

***

Let's see how it can be done:

Start your closing with your **THREE BEST POINTS**.

Summarise them.

Now go into the detail of the evidence, coming back to those three best points as part of the detail.

Finally, at your peroration repeat your three best points, in summary.

See, you've repeated your three best points three times.

A jury is likely to remember some of them, and hopefully all of them.

***

Three is always good.

Of course, it does not really apply to addressing judges, as was mentioned before in chapter eight.

If doing threes with a judge, you should not repeat a point three times, as you can expect the point to be comprehended first time.

However, as was mentioned before, what you can do is find three different ways of making the same point.

There is a difference.

***

When giving reasons for an argument to the jury, give three.

A witness is unreliable, vague, exaggerating.

A witness is solid, impartial, measured.

A defendant is lying, lying, lying.

A description was extreme, absurd, fanciful.

An expert was careful, cautious, helpful.

For reasons which are a mystery, supporting a point with three reasons sounds great, and carries weight, even if it shouldn't.

Threes give you momentum.

Like a wave, your words roll over the court.

You appear relentless, unstoppable, strong.

When jurors lose concentration, even if they hear just one of three reasons, they still follow your point, as the wave and flow of your words carries the jury, even if the other two reasons are missed, impressing upon them the correctness of the one reason they have remembered.

***

Threes are all about **RHYTHM**.

Be aware of it.

It can carry an audience.

Imagine you are sweeping them home, carrying them off, like leaves in a river.

A flow of words, like a flow of water, has direction.

Actors know this.

Even if not concentrating on your precise words, an audience can be swept to your bidding by the rhythm of your sentences and the engaging mesmerising projection of your voice and personality. You can carry them with flow alone.

***

When speaking,
remember,
remember,
remember,
VARY YOUR VOICE frequently, gently rising and falling with your points.

A varied voice is interesting to listen to—and you want the jury listening.

Speak quietly so the jury have to lean forward and concentrate to hear you. Then steadily louden your voice from your chest—not shouting. The force of your voice now presses upon their minds.

Undulate your sentences. Quicken them, slow them down.

Emphasise words, pause, emphasise another word, pause, quietly press to the end of the sentence, voice gently rising to the full stop.

Now pounce on the next sentence, ask a rhetorical question, voice rising with the question mark, and answer it, staccato-like, emphasising each word, with measured gesticulation.

Get the picture?

At least get this: don't be dull.

***

GESTICULATION can be a powerful tool.

Avoid dramatics like thumping tables.

Refrain from too much hand movement.

Do not plan it—it looks wooden.

But some gesticulation is allowed.

There is no rule which says to keep your hands firmly behind your back.

Just let it happen.

But when it does, ensure the gesticulation is **PURPOSEFUL RATHER THAN PLENTIFUL**.

***

PRACTICE, PRACTICE, PRACTICE your closing speech.

I'm not kidding.

Mirrors are good for this. It is a performance. Watch how you move, how you hold your head, what gesticulations naturally work.

If you can, get in front of a video camera at least once a year and get a good look at how you appear, and at what seems to work.

It's spooky but useful. You'll be amazed to see yourself. At first you will be embarrassed—but hey, it is better you are embarrassed in private than you embarrass the client in public. And as you work on how you appear, you will very, very quickly improve.

***

Listen to the sound of your words, and remember **FLOW, FLOW, FLOW**.

A speech should not be a treatise in scientific dispassion. It should bubble and swirl and froth.

Not excessively.

It should be about reaching inside the minds, and particularly inside the instincts of the jury or tribunal.

Closing should have a touch, just a touch, of drama.

It should have heart.

It should be restrained, with a hint of passion.

***

Criticism of witnesses should usually be **MORE IN SORROW THAN IN ANGER**.

Do not appear angry with a witness.

A jury will generally feel it is inappropriate for you to get righteous.

If attacking a witness, put your concerns in terms of how unfortunate it is that the witness has left himself wide open to attack. Suggest to the jury that one is sorry to have to say the witness was exaggerating or lying. These things sadly happen. They should not. But they do. The witness should have told the truth, but unfortunately in the theatre of court, with battle lines drawn, he has become biased and prone perhaps to overstate what he saw. It is understandable but most unfortunate that he is not accurate, is not reliable, and sadly, you may feel members of the jury, even not telling the truth.

Let the jury then be angry with the witness.

But as for you, they will think you a model of restraint.

***

Of course, the speech should be all about the evidence heard during the trial.

Never fall into the trap of appearing to give evidence or appearing to give your own opinion.

You can in fact do just a little bit of both, but there are rules.

***

Providing you refer to what may sensibly be thought by most to be within **COMMON KNOWLEDGE**, what you say is not a form of giving evidence.

You cannot tell the jury about the life cycle of a bruise in great medical detail if there has been no evidence of that medical detail; but you can observe that bruises do not appear immediately as a matter of common knowledge.

What is in common knowledge is a wide area. We can refer to famous films or books, to incidents in the news, and to the little irritations we all experience in shops or trains and on the Clapham omnibus.

The advantage of injecting these features into a speech is that the jurors identify with the advocate.

Hopefully, if it is done right, there is a sense of shared experience, outlooks, understanding, and values.

Instead of being a lawyer talking at them, you become a person sharing suggestions with them.

If they identify with you because of shared experience, a jury is more likely to agree with you.

***

A SHARED IMAGE from outside the evidence can be a powerful peg upon which to hang an important point.

If you can associate some key feature of the case with some clear image that everyone has seen, for example in a film, then you know exactly what that image is inside each juror's mind.

The image sown is not open to the vagaries of imagination in which each person sees something slightly different in their mind's eye.

To some extent, you have precise control over the jury's perception.

Let's consider an example. It may not be the best example, but it could help to set the idea.

Let us suppose it is important to convey to a jury how upset a mother was at being separated from her child, which then led to an alleged assault on a police officer. You might remind the jury of the desperately sad moment in Disney's *"Dumbo"*, when the little elephant is separated from his mother. Most people on the jury will have seen it, and many will have had tears in their eyes. You might remind them, carefully, oh very carefully, of that moment to help explain your defendant's feelings at what you say is the unthinking irrational moment you say she may have struck out in what she thought was defence of her frightened child being taken from her. Will anyone convict, no matter how hard the officer was clouted, if you have Dumbo playing in the mind of the jury?

But be sure the image fits and is not some cheap trick to hoodwink the jury. They will not like that.

Be careful how you introduce it.

It's often a question of feel and experience, but a shared image can be a powerful tool of persuasion.

***

Quotations can be a peculiar form of common knowledge. Everyone is assumed to know Shakespeare and the utterances of the great novelists, philosophers and politicians. But of course, they don't really.

BE CAREFUL OF QUOTATIONS.

They can sound pompous.

They are always best delivered as throwaway lines, rather than as heart-stopping utterances.

If a quotation works, a jury will know.

If it does not, as a throwaway line then the jury will forgive you.

But be careful.

My own view is don't try it until you have a few years experience. If it is uttered with the wrong emphasis, you lose respect, and if you lose respect, you fail to be persuasive.

***

Turning now to opinion, the golden rule is don't appear to give your own.

Notice the word *"appear"*.

It is all a question of how you do it.

Inevitably, a speech is an opinion.

But it has to be pitched right.

You dress up your opinion as comment—and then you invite the jury to consider the comment.

In other words, advocates use stock phrases like:

> *"You may feel that* . . . the defendant is lying"; or
> *"You are invited to consider* whether in light of the evidence the witness is mistaken".

Or

> *"You may think. . . "*
> *"It's a matter for you whether. . . "*
> *"It may be that your assessment is. . . "*

What you are in effect suggesting is an opinion to the jury that the defendant is lying and the witness mistaken. But of course it does not look or feel like that, because instead it is offered as the opinion of the jury, and not of the advocate.

I guess the short point here is: **OFFER OPINION TO THE JURY AS THEIRS NOT YOURS**.

***

Do not blunder into

> *"I believe. . . ",*
> *"In my opinion. . . ",*
> *"You should believe. . . ",*
> *"It is obvious that. . . ".*

A tribunal will jealously guard its right to decide a case. It will instinctively rebel against being told what your opinion is since your opinion ought to be irrelevant. The tribunal will feel it is only its own opinion that is important.

As I have said before, if you push, it will push back.

Frame everything as a delicate invitation.

So much of an effective speech is a question not simply of what you say, but of how you say it.

***

DO NOT ATTEMPT HUMOUR, unless you are very, very good.

It should always be a throwaway line, and it absolutely must fit the facts. If you step outside the facts to tell a joke, even a good joke, professionally you will drown in court.

Juries hate it. Any tribunal hates it. They think you are trying to hoodwink them by amusing them, and that you think they are stupid enough to follow you because you have entertained them.

***

One other thing: juries are not stupid.

Some people like to suggest they are. But they are not.

No way.

Ever.

They can become confused. But never stupid.

Individuals on a jury may be slow, but a jury of twelve is an organ which is much greater than the sum of its parts.

Collectively it sees everything, misses nothing, and has considerable wisdom.

Mark these words:

NEVER, NEVER, NEVER ASSUME A JURY HAS MISSED SOMETHING.

***

And on that point, because you must never assume the jury has missed something, **ADDRESS EVERYTHING** in your speech which may affect your case.

It is fatal to ignore some feature of the evidence because it was only mentioned once, is too difficult to deal with, mentioning it will only draw attention to it, and it may open a can of worms in the jury's mind.

No, no, no.

That can is already open and you must put the lid back on.

If you can see a problem, you can be sure they can.

And if you don't deal with the problem, they will know why—they will know it undermines your case and you have no persuasive answer, and so you will lose.

***

In the early stages of your career, as a rule of thumb, try to keep a speech to no more than **TWENTY MINUTES**.

Any longer, and we are likely to bore the jury, unless we have all the great delivery techniques.

Just a rule of thumb.

***

As another rule of thumb, **A CLOSING SPEECH SHOULD START WITH THE TEST**.

If prosecuting, say to the jury:

"The Crown invites you to say you are sure he knew he was carrying drugs. That is the test—are you sure. And the Crown invites you to say you can be sure for these three key reasons . . . " and off you go with your three best points, succinctly, quickly and clearly stated. "And when you consider these three points in evidence you may feel it is clear, it is obvious, applying the crucial test, you are sure he knew what he was carrying". Now you dive into the detail of the case, repeating your three best points as you go. And then perorate with them.

If defending, how about starting:

"In order to convict this man, you must be sure he knew he was carrying drugs. Sure. Not suspicious. Not probably knew. Sure. And if you feel he did not know, or may not have known, naturally and properly you would acquit. May not have known. In other words, is it reasonably possible he did not know. The defendant need prove nothing. The prosecution must prove its case. The prosecution must prove there is no reasonable possibility he did not know. Nonsense, when you consider these three points . . . " And off you go with your three best points. And then remind them of the test again. "In this case, sure means the total absence of a mere reasonable possibility. And I respectfully invite you to conclude that possibility is perfectly reasonable. You may feel you should acquit. Let us look at the evidence . . . "

***

If you start with the test, the jury measure everything you say against it.

It gives them direction and a framework in which to place the evidence.

And of course, at the end, it is usually best to remind the jury of the test and naturally of those three best points again, giving the tidy impression you have come full circle.

***

And finally, in every speech,

and always generally,

as was mentioned in the chapter on persuasiveness:

TELL A STORY,

KEEP IT SIMPLE,

SHOW THE WAY,

ASSIST, and

REMEMBER IRRESISTIBILITY.

***

CHAPTER XVII

MITIGATION

In crime, if defending, despite your best efforts, the jury may have convicted.

Perhaps the defendant has pleaded guilty.

The judge must now pass sentence, and will want to consider the mitigation.

Mitigation can be tricky.

The most important thing to remember above all else is **EYE CONTACT**.

You must look at the judge.

Here is raw power.

Your judge may imprison your defendant, separating him from family and friends, and leading to his employer sacking him, never more to have a good job. A life can be turned upside down.

In some cases, the hidden agenda in the mind of the defendant is not guilt, but sentence—he will not admit an offence for fear of jail.

You are what stands between that raw power and the defendant. Your responsibility is considerable.

So look at the judge. Not at the floor.

***

Often, mitigation is about putting an offence in a certain category.

We seek ways of **DISTINGUISHING OUR CASE** from other cases, or our defendant from co-defendants.

We might say a burglary is of commercial not domestic premises, and therefore less serious; in daylight and not at night, and therefore less serious; when premises were unoccupied, not occupied by the sleeping owners, and therefore less serious; the offence was spontaneous not premeditated; the window was open, not broken; and so on.

By **STATING WHAT THE OFFENCE IS NOT**, we often help the judge to place the offence within an appropriate bracket of seriousness.

**

CALL CHARACTER WITNESSES if possible, even sometimes where the defendant has previous convictions.

It is always helpful for a judge to have the measure of a defendant from what others apart from the advocate say about him.

In the absence of live witnesses, hand up references, particularly from work.

In fact, try to have references in addition to live witnesses.

***

LOOK UP THE LIKELY SENTENCE in *Current Sentencing Practice* by D. A. Thomas QC,

It is always, always sensible.

Many people fail to do this.

Even with experience, new cases present new challenges. Don't always assume your experience will carry you. It is so needlessly embarrassing to have suggested to a defendant he will receive less than is ordered.

While many fail to look up sentences, you can be sure the judge will—and it is obviously better to know what he will find.

***

KNOW WHEN TO STOP.

Often counsel begins with an excellent mitigation. The judge listens, swayed by the excellent delivery. However the advocate overdoes it, repeating some points, padding out others.

The judge's mind now wanders on to whether a good point really is such a good point, and in mild irritation at the length of the address, begins finding reasons to disagree.

Instead, **RUN EACH POINT THROUGH** like a swordsman, deliberately, not hurriedly, but solidly, withdraw your rapier, watching the judge for acknowledgement the point is fully taken, and now run the next point through.

List your points clearly.

Don't slash about, poking and prodding the same point, but never really killing it, or killing it too often—

One solid thrust, twist, and withdraw.

***

Finally, with deference, **TELL THE JUDGE WHAT SORT OF SENTENCE YOU SEEK AND WHY**.

Often mitigation is a tale of woe, but what sentence is sought is never expressed.

Review the sentencing options, explaining why each one is attractive.

Don't just leave it to the judge to decide.

And be **REALISTIC** in your suggestion.

You will damage your credibility if you seek a particular sentence which is wholly inappropriate, like community punishment for wounding with intent.

Without credibility, your whole mitigation will suffer.

Where appropriate, refer to a sentencing authority. It is surprisingly rarely done.

But why?

It seems obvious there should be more of it.

***

CHAPTER XVIII

THE COURT OF APPEAL

In the early years of practice, you will rarely go the Court of Appeal.

I don't propose to say much.

However, you will probably have some appearances, and they will terrify you.

Don't be frightened.

The Court of Appeal is fantastic. Their Lordships are extremely clever, and the papers are always fully considered before you get to your feet. They know exactly what they want to talk about, and usually will tell you straight away. And they are always courteous.

***

You will usually be over-prepared. You will have been up half the night trying to think of every permutation of question you might be asked, and every aspect of the facts of your case.

Try to relax.

Keep it simple.

While you may have prepared a long and detailed opening of the application, almost always you will not utter it. Their Lordships will interrupt you politely and take you straight to the point which interests them. Your appearance usually takes the form of questions and you do your best to answer them. It is like a moot. Simply keep your wits about you. You may be right in what you say. You may be wrong. But don't worry. That is why Their Lordships are there—to decide whether you are right.

Certainly, you should spend a little spare time sitting in the public gallery of the Court of Appeal, becoming familiar with the atmosphere and culture of the court.

**

Your guiding light is probably our chapter eight, although you can assume in the Court of Appeal, they do know the law, and a lot better than you. In fact, you will need to be well-read in the relevant law as they may of course be troubled by some fine point of distinction, and Their Lordships may not always agree among themselves on interpretation.

However the other points in chapter eight all still apply,

about speaking slowly,
with deference and politeness,
only needing to make a point once,
being brief,
making eye contact,
having prepared a short, opening statement which captures the heart of your application,
and weaving your skeleton into your argument.

Above all, enjoy the experience.

***

Chapter XIX

ADVOCACY IN INTERNATIONAL CRIMINAL COURTS

As at the date of this second edition, I have suspended my domestic London criminal practice and worked since October 2004 at two UN international criminal tribunals, have taught advocacy skills there, and to prospective defence advocates at the International Criminal Court, to the prosecution advocates at the War Crimes Court for Bosnia in Sarajevo, and in Cambodia, and have been a guest of the Prosecutor at the Special Court for Sierra Leone in Freetown.

International criminal courts are growing. They deal with genocide, crimes against humanity, and war crimes.

There are two ad hoc tribunals created by the UN in the 1990s—for the former Yugoslavia in The Hague (ICTY), dealing with the Balkan wars of the 1990s, and for Rwanda in Arusha, Tanzania (ICTR), dealing with the genocide of one million Tutsi in 1994.

There is also the more recent International Criminal Court (ICC), also sitting in The Hague, and which at the time of writing has yet to complete a trial.

Yet to convene is the Special Tribunal for Lebanon (STL) which may in time sit in The Hague and enquire into the assassination of Lebanese prime minister Rafik Hariri.

In addition, there are local courts with international input. Best known are the war crimes courts in Bosnia, Kosovo, Sierra Leone, Iraq, East Timor, and Cambodia.

I thought readers might like a taste of the advocacy challenges presented in these new international fora.

There are of course—you know me by now—ten.

***

The first challenge is *the mix of the inquisitorial with the adversarial style*.

In the UK, and throughout the US and the present and former Commonwealth, the court embraces adversarial advocacy. In serious cases, a judge rules on the law while the facts are mostly found by a jury. The presentation of evidence is controlled by the prosecution and by the defence. The issue is whether on the evidence presented the prosecution has proved its case beyond a reasonable doubt. Each side is allowed to cross-examine the other's witnesses, which means suggestions can be put in questioning.

On the continent of Europe, and throughout the former latin and francophone colonies, and former and present communist countries, the courts tend to embrace a more inquisitorial style. While there is prosecution and defence, the proceedings of law and evidence are completely controlled by the judge. He decides from a dossier of all information gathered on a case what evidence to hear live, and mostly controls what questions will be put to witnesses, often asking the vast majority of questions. Cross-examination is not allowed, as it is thought it might erroneously place suggestions in the mind of the witness. Essentially, the judge finds the facts, and is active in inquiring into the truth of a matter, asking himself whether a suspect who appears to be guilty is in fact beyond reasonable doubt guilty.

In international criminal courts, judges and lawyers are drawn from around the world from both systems. This daily creates very different perspectives on how best to proceed in trial.

Although there are some variations, the international system is essentially adversarial, with the prosecution and defence deciding what evidence shall be called. Cross-examination is allowed. However, the court is presided over by a bench of usually three judges, of sometimes mixed international and local background, which also find the facts.

Any advocate needs first and foremost to know the background of his three judges. In this way, submissions and questions can to some extent be tailored to the expectations of the bench.

In five trials in two tribunals, I have observed judges from Scotland, Jamaica, Korea, St Kitts in the Caribbean, Burkina Faso, Denmark, Ghana, Argentina, Pakistan, Norway, Sweden, the Czech Republic, Cameroon, and Kenya. Prosecution advocates with whom I have worked have been from the US, Nigeria, Jamaica, The Netherlands, Canada, South Africa, Botswana, Cameroon, Tanzania, Rwanda, India, Thailand, Uganda, The Gambia, New Zealand and Australia. Defence advocates have been from the US, Senegal, France, Cameroon, Canada, England, South Africa, Kenya, and Germany.

It's quite a mix, and is enormously interesting.

In fact, the mix makes it the best job in the world.

***

Time is precious in the courtroom, where events of magnitude are considered, and there is not enough time available to hear absolutely everything which might conceivably be relevant.

It is difficult to keep things short.

But this is what is needed—*keep the evidence as short as possible*.

The Rwanda genocide embraces three months of slaughter throughout the country. The Balkan troubles embrace four wars involving three countries and NATO in seven years.

Your average UK burglary or murder is usually one event relating to limited victims with limited defendants on limited dates. Such trials are generally short.

International trials are long. There is so much evidence that it is sometimes difficult to know where to start, what to say, and when to stop. Trials always last many months, and often years.

This means an advocate must have a good nose for what really matters, and what lies at the heart of a case, rather than what is interesting but peripheral. A trial should be about guilt, not history. These lines can blur.

AT ALL TIMES FOR AN INTERNATIONAL ADVOCATE, THE FOREMOST QUESTION IS:

> *If prosecuting, does this fact offer proof of guilt?*
> *If calling defence evidence, does it suggest innocence?*
> *If neither, exactly why call it?*

If the advocate is not sure, then it is generally not relevant.

It is not the other way around, namely I will call it unless I am sure I should not.

I repeat: *if the advocate is not sure, then it is generally not relevant*.

***

This is the second challenge—*determining what is relevant* in order to keep things short.

You must pay very careful attention to this. Often advocates prosecuting and defending work in teams, so that everyone's work is constantly reviewed by others. This can lead to advocates erring perhaps far too much on the side of caution for fear of criticism of colleagues. In this way they will hesitate to drop a fact from evidence in case someone else might think later it could have been helpful. As a result, a lot of irrelevant material ends up being sought, taking up valuable court time, and not determinative of any issue, but only offered so the advocate can . . . well . . . cover his back.

Remember courage. You need this.

Don't be afraid, after listening carefully to colleagues, nevertheless to stand by your judgment and drop material.

***

Because time is precious, *legal argument is almost always written*, so that court time can be taken hearing from witnesses.

The third challenge is therefore that there is a lot of writing.

A style of presentation has emerged.

A written motion begins by identifying a problem and asks for a remedy.

It then refers to the law. This can be found in a tribunal's rules of procedure and evidence and in the many authorities created by the Judgments and interlocutory Decisions of the international courts. Legal precedent in the ICTY and ICTR is mutually binding, as both share the same Appeals Chamber, while if international precedent is decided elsewhere it is considered persuasive.

The legal references must all be carefully footnoted.

The motion then discusses the facts of the problem and why the law fits the facts.

Finally, there is a prayer, seeking that the tribunal adopts the remedy sought.

The other side responds, which then leads to the applicant's reply. In time, the chamber issues a written decision.

Written advocacy takes up considerable time and often is required outside court sitting times, so that an advocate's working hours can be very long.

***

To my mind, the leading works on the jurisprudence of the international courts are:

>   *Archbold's* International Criminal Practice, and
>   *Blackstone's* International Criminal Practice.

There are many other works, while the jurisprudence is changing rapidly, yet these have collated the most information each in one work.

***

The fourth challenge is *the jurisprudence is voluminous and can be complicated*.

Judgments in trials and on appeal often run to hundreds of pages. And there are hundreds of interlocutory Decisions.

Indictments are long.

They lay out the charges, and often summarise facts in a growing jurisprudential legalese. There is not much in the style of an "opening note" where the bench is told a story as it is anticipated the evidence will emerge.

Usually, there are many charges which appear to allege pretty much the same thing. For example, genocide, conspiracy to commit genocide, complicity in genocide, and incitement to commit genocide. There are subtle differences, but what has emerged is an approach by jurists that the differences make the charges mutually different, when factually they overlap, and I do wonder whether less is more, and that we might simply charge less but more robustly.

Aiding and abetting is a specific mode of participation in an offence which is different to being the principal, whereas in the UK, that difference has been abolished, and is relevant only to sentence. Other modes, requiring separate pleading, are planning, instigating, ordering and committing an offence, or being a superior to others who participate in the above modes. I do wonder whether modes of participation ought to be less legalistic in the international courts. They are in essence simply the factual method of participation, and may not need to be so separately legal.

Another mode of participation is in a joint criminal enterprise, or JCE. It is difficult to define, as it refers to being a member of a group with a common criminal purpose, although how a defendant participates in that purpose is arguably without clear parameters.

The pleading of indictments has become very complicated. It may be that in time, there will be a return to greater simplicity. A good example of the trend toward the clarity of simplicity is the indictment against the former President of Liberia, Charles Taylor.

As for the judgments, long though they are, they are fascinating if heartbreaking—learn from them.

***

The fifth challenge is *document management*.

In international trials, truly colossal quantities of documents are available. Governments have often opened up their entire foreign office files to inspection. Reports from varieties of human rights groups multiply. Witness statements grow exponentially. There are video clips, radio broadcasts, and newspaper articles. In addition, there are copious previous and current trial transcripts. And there are military reports.

Then there are translations of all of the above, into French and English.

Three problems arise.

First, an advocate must be able to digest the relevance of lots of material very quickly. 'Nuff said.

Second, an advocate must be really good with the search engines available in a computer to sift the material into what is relevant. 'Nuff said.

Third, an advocate must know *how to use relevant documents in court*. This is not easy. The trouble is documents have to be prepared in their original form, with translations attached.

Paginated bundles are constantly necessary—fresh ones for each witness—to create ease of page reference to assist the bench, the parties, and the witness to follow the advocate.

Often when referring a witness to a document, the advocate refers to the page in the language of the witness, and must be able to refer to the page in the English and French translations for the judges. When a section of the document is read to the witness, if me, it is read from the English, while the witness follows from the document in his native language, yet what I am saying is *simultaneously translated* into French and then into the native language: well. . . you can end up with the simultaneous translation from my English being different when translated into the native language from what appears in the native language document, which can then cause all sorts of trouble.

Moreover, because of the delay in questioning created by simultaneous translation, a witness will often be reading other parts of the native document to what you are reading out, trying to get ahead of you, which can then lead to the witness not answering questions directly, instead trying to draw the attention of the court to what the witness finds interesting rather than the advocate.

The solution? You'll need lots of highlighters to cross-reference the same sections in the different translations. And above all, keep the section of a document put to a witness short, clear and unambiguous. Find the most relevant *sentence*, rather than read out a whole paragraph or page. The more you read out, the more likely things will go wrong.

***

The sixth challenge is *disclosure*.

This is a big area.

Different advocates from different jurisdictions have different attitudes to what to tell the other side. It can lead to distrust between the parties.

In general, the prosecution is required to disclose statements of its witnesses and anything possibly relevant and helpful to the defence. The grey area is: what is "possibly" relevant or helpful?

In general, the defence is required to disclose the identities of its witnesses, and while not a formal statement, something of what each will say. The grey area is how much is just enough of what each might say to satisfy the rule while giving away as little as possible.

Another problem is the sheer quantity of disclosure material which must be reviewed. It runs to literally millions of pages. If a party misses something, then if the other side learns it, the usual response is to suggest the ball is being hidden and that there is a measure of professional dishonesty rather than simple mistake.

Disclosure ends up causing lots of unnecessary rows.

Calling a witness is a big task: you need to have identified what is relevant and not peripheral to elicit in evidence, prepared your paginated bundles, thought about translation difficulties which may arise on important questions, and you need to have used your computer skills to ensure you have *reviewed all the important documents* and made *fair* disclosure decisions.

What's fair?

I respectfully suggest it is fair to *disclose everything unless there is positive reason not to*, rather than only disclose where there is positive reason to do so.

Give the other side the benefit of the grey.

Why? Because they will trust you and the trial will therefore run better.

And the judges will trust you too, thankful you have avoided endless tedious heated written disclosure arguments. They may think you wonderfully sensible, which will allow you later to be very persuasive indeed.

**

I have mentioned *simultaneous translation* and we need to consider this further

It makes a significant difference to witness examination in an international court.

Usually the language of the advocate is different from the language of the witness.

And sometimes from judges on the bench, and advocates opposite.

Sometimes even within your team.

Moreover, international courts usually as a matter of principle translate everything into English and French, being the official languages of the UN.

This means there are often three languages in play: I speak English, and am translated into both French and the local language. In the Rwanda tribunal, English goes into French, and from French into Rwandan, while the answer in Rwandan goes back into French and then into English.

It is not unusual to ask an open question, like "where did the massacre occur?" to which the answer coming back is "yes".

So you have to think.

You have to turn in your mind how the question might be translated, being sympathetic to the strain on the translators.

Is the question clear? Is it short? Is it unambiguous? If not, you lose control, because the witness may not hear the question you have asked, and answers something different.

Perhaps obviously, it is very useful to speak some French, and anticipate how the question will translate.

***

It follows the seventh challenge of international advocacy, where there is simultaneous translation, is *loss of questioning impact*.

There are two difficulties.

First, the question takes time to be translated, so that the relationship between an advocate and a witness is *distanced*. The questions and answers are often separated by an unconversationally-long period of time. *Rhythm* in the presentation of the evidence is lost.

Second, in cross-examination, the tone and nuance of a question is taken over by the translator, so that if putting something with direct robust steeliness, it may however be offered to the ear of the witness by the translator in an uncertain and sometimes hesitant tone, as the translator himself is uncertain of your meaning. The witness may now think you are asking for information, rather than using bounce, or putting an indisputable fact, so that the witness begins a discursive answer. *Control* over a cross-examined witness is tricky, and answers are more often longer in the international arena than domestically.

The solution, as in any domestic court, but perhaps ever more importantly in an international court, is to *keep questions short, clear and unambiguous*, so they can be quickly translated, with more of the advocate's tone more accurately conveyed, and consequently more quickly and concisely answered.

***

The eighth challenge can be *the intervention of the bench*.

In some trials the bench is reserved and allows the advocates to play out the evidence. In others, perhaps where the bench has judges from the inquisitorial school, there can be significant intervention during questioning.

Sometimes a judge becomes interested in a line of questioning and pursues it *proprio motu*. To an extent, the role of the advocate has been overtaken. A line from the bench might be pursued with open questions, which then become leading questions, and the line between direct and cross-examination can blur. An advocate needs to be alive to assisting the judge with the direction of his enquiry once permitted to resume control from the judge, while at the same time settling a witness who may otherwise have become surprised to have been engaging the bench directly. *All-round sensitivity* is the key.

***

The ninth challenge is *fitness*.

No kidding.

The volume of reading is huge. Then the hours in court are long—often the courts will sit from 9am to 5.30pm, with 90 minutes for lunch. Judges and advocates often address the court in French, requiring concentration if listening in French, and even more if listening to the English translation, which can sound disengaged from the speaker. Questioning witnesses while thinking of how questions may be interpreted and at the same time controlling the witness in the translation delay requires constant monitoring. Then after court, there is usually written work.

You have to be fit to get through it all.

And it's every day, with work at weekends.

So go to the gym.

***

And now to the tenth challenge—fraternisation.

It is unfortunate that generally in international courts the prosecution, defence, and bench do not often mix.

The bench is perhaps concerned that the advocates might seek indelicately to raise trial matters privately. And the advocates, coming from different professional backgrounds, and therefore not familiar with their opposition's different approaches, often fall out— little is agreed, with witnesses often unnecessarily called who might better have been read.

At the Bench and Bar of England and Wales, we have 700 years of fraternisation.

IT IS A GLORY.

Advocates learn from mixing with judges how the judicial mind works, that judges are real people too, and so an advocate's approach in court can improve and be better tailored to the expectations of the bench, speeding up the trial, and allowing readier persuasiveness.

Advocates learn from mixing with their opposition what problems beset each other, see each other's cases through each other's eyes, and learn to trust each other so that decisions can be taken mutually which assist the trial process. More than this, they improve their performance, they stretch themselves, by learning from each other, borrowing good ideas, and learning from the other what might be bad ideas. The robing room is a powerful and continuing university in the lifelong study of advocacy.

May I respectfully suggest **A CALL TO ARMS** to all from the London Inns of Court, no matter in which Commonwealth country you have then practiced: *if you are now before the international criminal courts, bring those 700 years of fraternisation with you*.

Arrange dinners and soirees, inviting the bench and opposition. Help our colleagues to feel comfortable with each other, and with the social and professional rules of entertaining the judges off the bench. I have had some modest fraternisation success at the Rwanda tribunal, working closely with two other members defending from the English Bar. Let's keep it up.

Spread the word, and help spread our glorious tradition.

***

Finally, if you find yourself in an international court, please let me know—it's a small world and readers of *The Devil's Advocate* should know each other, and so form an unofficial robing room, through email and calls, in which to continue to test ideas and improve our skills.

CHAPTER XX

IMPROVING ADVOCACY

When practicing to improve your advocacy, there is a well-tested system for constructive feedback from others. It was pioneered in the USA and has been exported throughout the world. It can be found in Canada, Scotland, New Zealand, Australia, India, Hong Kong, South Africa, Ireland and elsewhere. It has been used for training at the international courts, particularly the ICTY, the ICTR and the ICC. In 1994, it was finally imported from Australia to the English Bar by Justice George Hampel of the Victoria Supreme Court, and ever since has been the foundation of formal advocacy training within the Inns of Court.

It is very simple. But it works wonders.

In this book, we will call it **THE ONE POINT DEMONSTRATION**.

***

In an ideal world, students of advocacy will receive training in this method from their professional governing body. However, the basics of the method are not tricky or mysterious, and can be used between friends. Be careful of developing a bad technique. But practising something is surely better than doing nothing.

So have a go. Carefully.

Gather some colleagues. For each exercise, one is a witness, one is the advocate, one is a reviewer. The others just watch.

Use an old witness statement from an old case. Or make one up.

The advocate examines the witness for no more than five minutes. It can be examination in chief, cross-examination, anything. Throughout the exercise, the reviewer writes down *the questions asked, not the answers given*.

The reviewer then performs a one-point demonstration by following six steps.

No straying. Six steps. No more. No less. No variations. No padding it out. No waffle.

SIX STEPS.

***

So here is how it works.

You are the reviewer.

The first step is to identify **ONE POINT** on which to review.

Only one.

There may be hundreds, but we must stick to one point, and capture it bullishly in a single short sentence which we call the **HEADNOTE**. For example *"I want to talk to you about keeping non-leading questions short and simple during examination in chief"* or *"I want to talk to you about controlling answers in cross-examination."*

The headnote has to be short, pithy, and to the point. It must not be a treatise. Above all it must be **MEMORABLE** so that at the end of the review, and at the end of the day, and at the end of the next day, and at the end of next month, the advocate can be asked *"what was your headnote?"*, and he will remember.

***

The second step is to read back the questions asked by the advocate that you believe has led to the problem you have identified in the headnote.

We call this the **PLAYBACK**.

It is an odd thing to record the questions of the advocate, when so much of a lawyer's training is to record the answers of the witness. It takes a little practice.

Please note that it is important to have a careful note of the precise words used in the questions, otherwise the advocate will often dispute your accuracy and therefore will dispute the validity of your assessment of any problem.

Playback does not always have to be a record of questions asked. The head-note could be about body posture or nervous habits. The playback would then be a short demonstration of the posture or habit.

Whatever it is, it must accurately reflect what the advocate did or said.

***

We now explain why what was done does not work.

It is the third step and we call it the **REASON**.

The reason is often obvious. But don't skip this step. It focuses the mind.

It tells the advocate why there was a problem.

Interestingly, it also tells the reviewer why there was a problem, and helps him articulate what up until then, he may have only understood instinctively. Understanding something instinctively is no good when reviewing advocates—you have to be able to explain your instinct. And so the reason helps both the advocate and the reviewer toward a better understanding of advocacy.

***

Next comes the fourth step, the **REMEDY**, in which we explain how to put the problem right.

Often, this is not obvious. You have to know your stuff.

Think about it.

It is no good saying something does not work, and why.

What we need now is what will work and why.

What will work?

How do you put right the mistake you have identified?

How?

Think about this.

In the reason, you explain the problem. In the remedy, you explain the solution.

Often, the remedy is not easy, but at least it will have you thinking.

***

I want to keep talking about the remedy.

The one point demonstration is not just about identifying problems. It is about providing solutions. The exercise is pointless without a solution. Just saying something does not work is completely useless. Completely. Useless. It is the solution we want.

I've said it again on this page because it is really important.

Most people can tell you there is a problem. But not many can tell you how to put it right.

So let's use an example with the four steps so far.

Let's quote an imaginary review.

"My headnote is this: I want to talk to you about how you must always ask leading questions in cross-examination.

In my playback, I remind you that you asked the following three questions:

> *Where was the gun?*
> *How often was it fired?*
> *Was anyone hurt?*

The reason for always asking leading questions in cross-examination is it gives greater control over the witness who may otherwise answer open questions unpredictably.

The remedy is to tell the witness what you want the witness to say, one fact at a time, and add words to the effect of 'that's right isn't it?' at the end, so turning the statement into a question, like so:

> *The gun was in John's hand, wasn't it?*
> *It was fired three times, wasn't it?*
> *Joe was hit with three bullets in the head, wasn't he?*

Let me demonstrate the questioning. . . ."

***

And so we come to the fifth step, the **DEMONSTRATION**.

Having explained how to put the problem right, you now *show how it is done*.

This means the review is not some airy-fairy lecture. It has visual impact which can later be emulated. The review is not theory: it is practice. It is not dry and boring. It has life, and the advocate will always be able to recall in his mind's eye a visual presentation of how the problem is cured, because it has been demonstrated.

Demonstrations are a tricky business. You now really, really have to know your stuff. They can go wrong! You have to be prepared for embarrassment. Some senior advocates will run a long way from any risk of embarrassment. Don't let them off the hook. Senior advocates have a lot to teach. Encourage them to risk the embarrassment and help the profession.

Tell them, every time: *show me*.

***

The advocate finally repeats the demonstration in the sixth step which we call the **REPLAY**. The lesson is firmly learnt.

The replay lasts only a minute or so. It is designed for the advocate to get a feel for the solution, and not just to hear it or see it.

The advocate emulates the demonstration. By doing it, the solution is absorbed, rather than simply noted.

***

And not just by the advocate.

It is learned by those watching as well.

This is really important—with this method, those watching can learn just as much as those doing.

One point at a time. Demonstrated lessons firmly learnt by all.

Try it, and tell me I'm wrong.

***

Here is a summary of the one point demonstration technique:

Step 1:   Head-note   — "I want to talk to you about one point . . ."

Step 2:   Playback   — "The point arises because of these questions/actions . . ."

Step 3:   Reason   — "The reason this does not work is . . ."

Step 4:   Remedy   — "Here's how you put it right"

Step 5:   Demonstration   — "Watch me"

Step 6:   Replay   — "You try now".

Advocacy should be presented for no more than 5 minutes.

A review should last no more than 5 minutes.

Improvement is as good as guaranteed.

***

Please note you can use the one point demonstration to improve all aspects of advocacy. It need not be limited to witness exercises. An advocate can offer for review an opening speech, or a closing speech, or a legal argument supported by a skeleton.

The one point demonstration will work very effectively for all aspects of courtroom skills.

But remember to stick to the six steps.

***

One other thing—**USE A VIDEO CAMERA**.

Many people have one now. Or can borrow one.

Make a speech to camera, play it back, and wince.

Look at how others see you. It can be a bit of a shock. But learn from it.

Identify what you don't like about yourself, about your posture, about putting hands in your pockets, about tics, scratches, rocking to and fro, about looking slightly mad. . . and change it.

Record your advocacy on a video during a one point demonstration review. And then look at the performance. Get a colleague to look at it too. See what the colleague thinks. See what you think.

A video recording is a powerful learning tool. You can see what you don't like and do something about it. It allows you that rare if embarrassing treat—to see yourself as others see you.

***

If you do not arrange one-point demonstrations privately among your colleagues, and if you do not put yourself on camera, then what's left?

What's left is constructive criticism of your performance in **COURT**.

By whom?

By your opponent.

By other advocates who were in the well of the court.

But there is a problem here. Advocates usually feel it inappropriate to offer constructive criticism to each other. It is thought cheeky.

Unfortunately, this means there is a vast army of lawyers out there who have rarely ever been reviewed. Bad habits become entrenched, obvious for all the world to see, but no one dares say anything.

The solution is simple: **ASK THE OTHERS WHAT THEY THINK**.

Certainly there will be crushing and sometimes pompous criticisms from advocates whose own skills you don't rate particularly highly. However, generally speaking, the criticism of other advocates is measured and extremely helpful. It should be actively sought. We don't have to agree with it all the time. But it provides that crucial understanding of how others see us, and of what works and what doesn't.

So ask.

And then you can walk away, unlikely to see your reviewer for some time, so that the pang of any mild embarrassment is unimportant when weighed against the fact you have learned something.

***

It cannot be stressed enough how important it is to seek the judgment of others.

Pupil barristers and trainee solicitors are rarely seen in action in court by their pupil masters and principals.

It really is a tiptop idea while still junior with little precious status to lose, to ask what others at court thought, and to set up in chambers or the office regular one-point demonstration workshops.

A junior has very little to lose, but by **STEALING ALL THE BEST IDEAS** from seniors, by allowing them to teach you, ascent up the slippery slope of advocacy excellence can be rapid indeed. Techniques and ideas which a senior by trial and error took years to perfect, can be taught in an early evening.

It is crazy for advocates to improve advocacy entirely alone all their lives.

Have the courage to risk making a fool of yourself in front of others and the rewards will be many and immediate.

***

Chapter XXI

THE OVERALL ADVOCATE

And so we reach the end of this polemic. I don't intend to write a long, flourishing peroration. The last chapter will be a simple single page. The page will define the overall advocate, the person you should be, or becoming, after carefully considering the ideas here.

***

The overall advocate has judgement.

And

> poise,
> eye contact,
> common sense,
> good relations with the opposition,
> good questioning technique,
> and a great closing speech,
> which has been written long before the trial begins,
> and always tries to think like the tribunal, not so much the client.

And he is a credit to the profession if he is polite and he makes the tribunal really, really think about his case.

Above all, in everything he does in court, whether it is

> addressing the judge,
> questioning a witness
> addressing a jury,

he seeks that rare quality of irresistibility,
which makes him look almost invisible,
as if the case solved itself.

He is not a gladiator.

He remains himself and does not try to be someone he is not.

This sort of advocate will very often win.

Will this be you?